The Classic Guide to King Arthur

by

Dr Keith Souter

GGP

First published in the UK in 2012 by Golden Guides Press Ltd.

10 8 6 4 2 1 3 5 7 9

A CIP catalogue record for this book is available from the British Library.

ISBN (paperback) 978-1-78095-006-8
ISBN (Kindle) 978-1-78095-033-4
ISBN (ePub) 978-1-78095-034-1

Typeset in Palatino by Mac Style, Beverley.
Cover design by Mouse Mat Design Ltd.
Edited by Kathy Martin.
Printed and bound in the UK.

Golden Guides Press Ltd
P.O. Box 171
Newhaven
E. Sussex
BN9 1AZ
UK

admin@goldenguidespress.com
www.goldenguidespress.com

THE
CLASSIC GUIDE TO

King Arthur

BY
Dr Keith Souter

For my son, Andrew, a fellow Arthurian enthusiast.
May all your quests be successful.

Contents

Acknowledgements

It has been a pleasure to work on *The Classic Guide to King Arthur* and there are several people that I would like to thank for helping me in this adventure.

Firstly, I would like to thank Fiona Shoop, the editorial director at Golden Guides Press for giving me the opportunity to write a book about this archetypal monarch. Her advice in several areas was of inestimable help.

My agent Isabel Atherton at Creative Authors was her usual whirlwind of efficiency and I am grateful to her as always.

Kathy Martin, my editor has been a joy to work with and whenever she has wielded her editorial pen it has always been for the best.

Thank you also to Matthew Blurton at Mac Style for designing the book. He has made a handsome job of it.

I also thank all of the writers and artists, past and present, famous or not so famous, and also those great anonymous writers from antiquity for their parts in developing the wonderful, rich Arthurian œuvre.

And finally, thanks to my wife Rachel for her continued support. She makes everything worthwhile.

Introduction

THE STORIES about King Arthur and his Knights of the Round Table have been told and written about for centuries. They have been retold, translated into countless languages, filmed, serialised and adapted into ballet, opera and plays. Although they are set in Britain and epitomise the age of chivalry, yet they have an almost global and timeless appeal.

The stories tell of a heroic warrior king who forms a society of knights who are all bound by a strict code of honour to right wrongs, defeat evil and protect the meek, the mild and the downtrodden. No request for help would ever be turned down by them and each knight would rather die than have his honour besmirched.

King Arthur is not merely a ruler who inherits a throne, but one who is singled out and shown by mystical means to be the only true king. By drawing a sword from a stone, which no other knight has been able to do, it is clear that he possesses qualities which mark him out as the worthiest of knights, as a king who will lead his subjects wisely and bring light to the darkness that has engulfed the land.

The great Welsh wizard Merlin plays a not insubstantial part in the Arthurian stories. It is he who puts the sword in the stone and who guides Arthur in the early part of his reign, before he is bewitched into eternal sleep by Viviene, a sorceress of prodigious power.

There is ancient magic in the tales, such as is described in the way that Arthur is given his great sword

King Arthur.

Excalibur by the Lady of the Lake. None can resist this sword, which was given to him together with a scabbard which confers invulnerability upon him. That is a great gift, of course, yet when it is stolen from him he becomes as mortal as any of his subjects, which of course indicates that one day Arthur will perish through treachery.

The Round Table fashioned by Merlin's magic becomes symbolic of chivalry as does the very name of Camelot, the castle that houses it and which is home to King Arthur, Queen Guinevere and the Knights of the Round Table.

The Arthurian legends form the blueprint for many of the tales of heroes and heroism that have been told around the world. Yet the legend about the king, the knights and the various quests are themselves archetypal stories that revolve around concepts of good and evil, chivalry, loyalty, self-sacrifice, betrayal and treachery. They illustrate how human frailties and desires can undermine and ultimately destroy an edifice based like Camelot upon honourable principles.

The stories of King Arthur and his Knights of the Round Table stir emotions in all who hear them. They seem timeless. Yet is it fair to say that they are simply stories? Indeed it is a brave person who writes them off as such. For centuries it was assumed that Arthur had actually been the king of not just England, but of Britain. Even today a large proportion of the population would probably tell you that he was an actual historical person. Certainly, most people would be able to give a thumb-nail description of him, his knights and of Merlin, the great wizard. On the other hand, far fewer people would be able to describe or date about fifty per cent of the sovereigns who have ruled the land, even though so much has been documented about their reigns.

The field of Arthurian studies is huge and there is a vast amount of research that has been done in academic institutions and societies all over the world. Academics have forged long careers in the study of various aspects of the legends, the writings and the sources. Historians try to identify battlegrounds and possible Arthurian sites. Archaeologists search and excavate to try to find tangible evidence for the existence of a warrior called Arthur.

In this book we will look at all aspects of this great saga. We will look at the legend itself, the literary and historical roots for the stories and meet along the way many of the knights, queens, damsels and villains who people the legends. We shall meet some of the people who wrote about him and who helped to create the legend. We will see how the legacy of King Arthur and his knights forged the very foundations of chivalry throughout England and Europe and had such a profound influence upon many of the subsequent real kings and queens of England. We shall even see how the whole tale of Camelot found its allegorical counterpart in the administration of John Fitzgerald Kennedy, the 35th President of the USA. In addition, we will consider how the Arthurian legend influenced English literature, art and sculpture and how Arthur and his knights even formed the basis for the superheroes of popular culture today.

So come with us now. Let us part the mists of time and seek out King Arthur, Merlin and Sir Lancelot. All that you want to know about these timeless characters is contained in the pages of *The Classic Guide to King Arthur*.

Part One

King Arthur and his Knights of the Round Table

The basic tale

A S WE shall see as we wend our way back through time in our quest to know more about King Arthur and his Knights of the Round Table, there are several versions of the tales. Indeed, various integral components of the legend that most people know about were added by different writers over the centuries. These were all drawn together in the Fifteenth Century by a fascinating fellow called Sir Thomas Malory when he effectively wrote the first English novel, *Le Morte d'Arthur* which was published by William Caxton in 1485. It is upon this work that the following thumb-nail outline of the story of King Arthur is based. Later in the book we shall look at how subsequent writers added to it.

The Round Table.

Chapter One

The Tale of King Arthur

After that I had accomplysshed and fynysshed dyvers hystoryes as well of contemplacyon as of other hystoryal and worldly actes of grete conquerours and princes...the noble hystorye of the Saynt Greal and of the moost renomed Crysten kyng, first of the chyef of the thre best Crysten, and worthy, kyng Arthure, whyche ought moost to be remembred emonge us Englysshemen tofore al other Crysten kynges.

Preface to Sir Thomas Malory's
Le Morte d'Arthur, *William Caxton, 1485*

Merlin

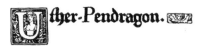

LONG ago, in the dark days after the Romans left Britain, King Vortigern tried to stave off attacks from the Picts and the Scots by seeking aid from Saxons from across the North Sea. The Saxons were mighty warriors and they came in their long boats and helped Vortigern to drive the northern invaders back. Among them were two brothers, Horsa and Hengist. Yet so beautiful did these warriors find the land that instead of returning to their home lands of Germany and Denmark, they sent word back, the result being that they came in increasing numbers and fought the Britons for their lands.

Vortigern in despair died and left Briton at the mercy of the invaders

Uther Pendragon, from *The Story of King Arthur and his Knights* by Howard Pyle, 1903.

12

who gradually pushed the Britons westwards towards Wales and the lands of Cornwall.

At last, a warrior king from the south called Uther Pendragon rose against them and rallied his neighbouring lords. He fought many battles with the Saxons and drove them back, thus bringing peace to the southern lands that he ruled over. Yet although he brought peace, his sovereignty was not accepted by all. There were several powerful lords who jealously guarded their lands and refused to acknowledge him as king. Chief among these was Gorlois, Duke of Cornwall, who had fought by Uther's side in the fiercest of battles against the Saxons.

Pendragon – the royal family name

Uther had taken the name of Pendragon because a great comet shaped like a dragon's head had been seen in the sky on the eve of a battle against the Saxons.

In an attempt to gain control over the kingdom King Uther summoned Gorlois, the Duke of Cornwall to Camelot, his great castle and centre of his realm, bringing with him his wife, the fair Igrayne, who was famous for her beauty and her wisdom. The moment Uther saw Igrayne he fell in love with her and determined to possess her. He contrived to get her alone and whispered his intentions in her ear. She was horrified and immediately ran to her husband and informed him of what Uther had said. Gorlois left in a rage, cursing the king for so besmirching the ideals of knighthood and honour.

Uther promised to wage war against Gorlois, who placed Igrayne in his impregnable castle at Tintagel for her safety while he garrisoned his other stronghold, Castle Terrible, and prepared to withstand a siege.

During the siege that lasted for fifty days and nights Uther fell sick as a result of his anger with Gorlois and his love for Igrayne. Uther's counsellor Sir Ulfius suggested that he send for Merlin, the enchanter, for only he could help.

In due course, Merlin mysteriously arrived and agreed to help Uther, but only if he granted him a single wish. The deal was struck and Merlin cast a spell which enabled Uther, Ulfius and himself to take on the appearance of Gorlois and two of his counsellors. Thus disguised they went to Tintagel and gained entrance. That night Uther slept with Igrayne and Arthur was conceived.

Merlin's part of the deal was that any child born of their union should be given to him.

The daughters of Gorlois and Igrayne

The Duke and Duchess of Cornwall had three daughters:

- Morgawse, who would marry King Lot of Orkney; later in the tale she would sleep with her half-brother King Arthur and give birth to Mordred, who would bring about the death of Arthur
- Elaine who would marry King Nantres of Garloth
- Morgan le Fay, the youngest child, who was sent to a nunnery where she was schooled in magic; she was Arthur's half-sister and his enemy who stole the scabbard of Excalibur

---

Gorlois was killed in battle and the nobles suggested that King Uther should marry Igrayne. Once married, Uther confessed that the child she was carrying was actually his, for it was he that she had slept with at Tintagel. When the child was born it was given into Merlin's care. He delivered the infant Arthur into the care of the good knight Sir Ector and his wife, who brought him up with their own son, Kay.

Two years later Uther was poisoned and the realm fell once again into disarray as the nobles fought among themselves. The Saxons grabbed their opportunity and started pillaging, gradually seizing more of the land of the Britons. There was need of a strong leader to save the country.

The two swords

Merlin reappeared from the wilds and conferred with the Archbishop, and together they called for a meeting of the lords in London on Christmas Day. While they were attending a service in the Abbey, a slab of marble mysteriously appeared with an iron anvil imbedded in it. Thrust deeply into the anvil was a sword with the handle pointing to the sky. Upon the stone was written:

Whoso pulleth this sword from this stone and anvil is the true-born king of all Britain.

No one present could remove the sword despite all their efforts. The Archbishop suggested that ten knights should guard it and that a further meeting and joust should be held on New Year's Day. When that day arrived, Sir Ector, his newly knighted son Kay and young Arthur travelled for the joust. On the way from their lodgings Sir Kay found that he had forgotten his sword so Arthur was despatched to get it. Unfortunately, the lodgings were locked. Then Arthur remembered the sword in the stone so he went to the churchyard where the sword in the anvil had been left unguarded, for all the knights had gone to the joust. He plucked it easily from the anvil and rode back to give it to Sir Kay.

Sir Kay recognised it and assumed that since he was now the owner of the sword, he must be the king. Sir Ector realised otherwise and all three returned to the churchyard where he ordered Arthur to put the sword back in the anvil. Once there, first he and then Kay tried, unsuccessfully, to remove it. Then Arthur was told to remove it, which he did easily. Sir Ector then told Arthur that he was the true king, explaining that he was only his surrogate father, his real father having been King Uther Pendragon. All that Sir Ector asked of Arthur was that he should make Sir Kay his seneschal.

But the nobles were not willing to accept a beardless boy as their king, so a decision was put off until Candlemas, at the beginning of February. At Candlemas still none of the nobles could remove the sword, and once again Arthur did so easily. Yet again they refusd to reach a decision and deferred it until Easter, and then again when none but Arthur could remove the sword they delayed it until Pentecost.

On this final occasion the people of London agitated and cried out that there should be no more delay, for they accepted Arthur as their king. The

The sword in the stone (Bretton laRoche).

majority of the nobles willingly accepted him, but some did so only with reluctance.

Arthur gave the great sword to the Archbishop and was created the First Knight of the realm and, soon after, was crowned King of England. He then set about leading his people against the Saxons and won many victories.

Still, however, there remained nobles who refused to accept Arthur's sovereignty. These included King Lot of Orkney and King Nantres of Garloth, who were married to two of his half-sisters. They threatened to rise against him, so Merlin advised him to go to Caerleon in South Wales, to a great tower that would be able to withstand a siege. When the kings arrived with their armies Merlin tried to negotiate on Arthur's behalf, but at last there was no alternative but for Arthur to leave the tower and fight. He advised Arthur to fight with another sword, however, and only to use the sword that he drew from the stone if he seemed to be losing the battle. This he did and the sword drawn from the stone glowed like the sun as he cut a swathe through his foes who fell down and finally accepted him as their king.

Shame, a dream and the Questing Beast

Although he had expressed loyalty, yet King Lot was still envious of Arthur. He sent his wife, Morgawse and her four sons to court. Her purpose was to spy on Arthur, which she did by seducing him. In fairness, Arthur was willingly seduced but at that time he was unaware that he had slept with his half-sister. From their incestuous union Mordred, the knight who would bring about Arthur's death, would be born. Yet he would not know him as his son, but as his nephew.

Afterwards Arthur had a dream in which his land was ravaged by griffins and serpents. They killed and consumed all his people and then turned on him. He defeated them, but only at a terrific cost to himself for he almost died from his many wounds. When he awoke he was confused and shocked by the dream and went hunting to try to divert his mind.

He saw a deer and chased it but it was too nimble and kept evading him. Then his horse collapsed and he sent a yeoman to get him another mount. As he waited he heard a mighty noise, like a whole pack of dogs. Then a monstrous beast came out of the forest. It was part lion, part

---

The sons of King Lot and Queen Morgawse

They would have four sons, all of whom would prove worthy Knights of the Round Table:

- Sir Gawain – a true and good knight who would have many adventures of his own, including one recounted in the great medieval poem *Sir Gawain and the Green Knight* which was not part of Malory's work
- Sir Gaheris – who would die by Sir Lancelot's hand
- Sir Agravaine – who would conspire against Sir Lancelot and Queen Guinevere
- Sir Gareth – another great knight who would die by Sir Lancelot's hand

---

hound, part horse and part serpent. After his dream he thought that it would attack him but it ignored him and went to drink at the nearby spring, then made off into the forest again.

The Questing Beast, by Henry Justice Ford, from *King Arthur, Tales of the Round Table*, 1904.

Arthur fell asleep by the spring and was awoken some time after by a knight. He told Arthur that he was King Pellinore and that it was his fate to pursue the Questing Beast. Unfortunately, he had lost his horse. Just then the yeoman returned with a fresh horse for Arthur and King Pellinore asked him to let him have the horse. Arthur declined but offered to take over the quest for him. King Pellinore vaulted onto the horse and told him that only he or, should he die on the quest, his son, Sir Palomides could hope to capture it. Arthur remonstrated and said that they should fight but Pellinore said that he must continue the quest, and

17

if Arthur desired to fight he should meet him at his pavilion in the forest and bang on his shield which would be hanging from a tree.

While Arthur awaited another horse, Merlin came to him in the form of a fourteen year old boy and told him that he knew about the Questing Beast and also many things about him. Arthur refused to believe him and chased him away. Soon after, Merlin returned in the form of an old man. They talked and he revealed that he was the fourteen year old boy. He then told Arthur that he had committed a great sin by sleeping with Morgawse, his half-sister, and that the child from their union would one day destroy him and all that he held dear. Yet he would not reveal who that child was, for it was not something that he was permitted to know. Merlin then prophesied his own end, telling Arthur that he would be buried alive.

Later, Arthur met King Pellinore and jousted with him but was overcome by the older knight. He was on the point of being killed when Merlin appeared and cast an enchantment upon Pellinore, causing him to fall asleep. Arthur was mortified that enchantment had been used to help him, for he feared that Merlin's magic had slain a mighty and noble knight such as he had never fought before. But Merlin told him that it must be so and that Pellinore would be of value to him and that he would have two sons who would be of inestimable value in later years. These sons were Sir Percival and Sir Lamorak of

---

The Questing Beast

This is a creature that is named in different versions of the tale. In early versions it is a small creature like a fox, but in Malory's *Le Morte d'Arthur* and in T.H. White's *The Once and Future King* it is a real chimera. It had an unholy birth, possibly from the conception of a child by the shape-shifting devil.

In this version, which is in keeping with the legends as illustrated in this book, it has the head of a serpent, the body of a leopard, the hindquarters of a lion and the feet of a hare. It is not easy to find, of course and the 'quest' refers partly to the hunt for it but also to the braying noise that it makes, as if it has forty braying or questing dogs in its stomach.

Wales. More than that, King Pellinore would tell him the name of his son by Morgawse.

The Lady of the Lake and the sword

Merlin took Arthur to a hermitage where a hermit skilled in healing cured him of his wounds. When Arthur recovered he was downcast because he had no sword. Merlin told him not to worry, for a sword had been prepared for him. He took him to a lake and showed him a strange sight. A sword emerged from the water clasped in the hand of a woman. A barge came out of the mist with a lady standing in it.

This, Merlin told him, was the Lady of the Lake. She told Arthur that he may take the sword if he promised to grant her a wish when she asked it. He agreed and paddled out and took the sword and its scabbard. Immediately the hand sank back into the water and the Lady of the Lake disappeared.

Merlin asked Arthur which he preferred, sword or scabbard. When Arthur said he liked the sword better, Merlin told him his choice was

The Lady of the Lake gives Excalibur to King Arthur, by Alfred Kappes, 1880.

poor, since as long as he wore the scabbard not a drop of blood would he lose.

Arthur's black deed

Merlin had told Arthur that the child who would be his undoing would be born in May. Arthur therefore decreed that all male babies born in May to any of his lords or knights should be surrendered to him. When they were – including Mordred who was born to Queen Morgawse, King Lot of Orkney's wife – Arthur had them all put aboard a ship and cast adrift. Their lives were left to the foibles of the sea. As it happened, the ship was caught in a storm and was shipwrecked with the loss of many lives. Mordred was saved, however, and was brought up by a good man until he was fourteen, when he was presented at Camelot and duly knighted. The stage was thus set for tragedy to happen.

Balin – or the Knight with Two Swords

King Arthur received a message from King Ryan of North Wales demanding homage from him. King Ryan had previously received tribute from eleven other kings and from each of these kings he had cut off a portion of their beards to make a border for his mantle. He threatened that if Arthur did not comply, he would attack and cut off not only his beard, but his head also. Arthur sent a message back to Ryan that he was declaring war on him and would have his head.

A damsel then came to court with a request that a good and true knight without sin should help her. The task, she said, removing her cloak to show a sword strapped to her side, was to remove a sword from its scabbard. The sword, she told the king, had been sent by the Lady of Avalon.

Neither Arthur nor any of his knights could remove it. Then Balin, a young knight who had recently arrived in Camelot but had yet to prove his worth, did so with ease. When the lady asked for the return of the sword he refused to let her have it, so enchanted by it was he. Then the damsel left after telling him that the sword was cursed and it would be his downfall and his great sorrow.

Not long after she left, another lady came to the court. It was none other than the Lady of the Lake. She talked with Arthur and told him that the sword he received from the lake was called Excalibur, meaning steel-cutter. She then reminded him of their bargain. Her request was to have the head of the knight who removed the sword the other lady brought. The sword had apparently been stolen by the first lady.

Balin heard all this and his temper flared. He drew the sword and cut off her head, to the horror of all present. King Arthur sent him away from court for the dishonour that he brought by his act, telling him never to return unless he redeemed himself. Balin departed, determined to regain the king's favour, so he set out with the intention of killing King Ryan. Ever after, he was known as the Knight with Two Swords.

Merlin explains about the cursed sword

King Arthur had the Lady of the Lake buried with honour as befitted her rank. Not long after this, Merlin returned to court and was told about Balin, the sword and the death of the Lady of the Lake. He then told King Arthur that the damsel who brought the sword had been deceitful and was wicked. She had a lover who had been killed in fair combat by her own brother, who was a good and worthy knight. In anger and eaten away with a desire for vengeance she had asked the Lady of the Lake to help her take revenge on her brother. The Lady of the Lake gave her the sword and told her that whoever could remove it from its scabbard would kill her brother, and would himself be killed.

The first victims of the curse

One of King Arthur's young knights felt incensed at the dishonour that Balin had brought upon the court and asked the king for permission to pursue and challenge him to combat. The king agreed.

This knight, Sir Launceor, a prince of Ireland, overtook Balin and challenged him, the two fighting until Balin ran him through with his sword. As he leant over the valiant knight a young damsel rode up. She was in love with Sir Lanceor, as was he with her. "Sir Balin," she cried, "you have killed two hearts with that one blow." And so saying she attempted to stab herself with a dagger. But Balin grabbed it from her, only to see her pick up his discarded sword, turn it round and fall upon it. In horror at the death of the lovers he rode away.

A meeting with his brother and with Merlin

His heart full of sadness, Balin met another knight who was none other than his own brother, Sir Balan. Balan listened sympathetically to Balin's tale and offered to ride with him to overcome King Ryan.

Along the road they met an old man who revealed himself as Merlin. He told Balin that he had done himself great harm, for he should have prevented the damsel's suicide. "Because of the death of that lady you will strike the most dolorous stroke since our Lord Jesus Christ suffered."

When Balin asked for more information Merlin disappeared and the two brothers rode on. Again Merlin appeared and informed them that soon King Ryan and sixty knights would be heading their way.

The Dolorous Stroke

Jesus Christ was stabbed in the side as he hung upon the cross. The weapon used belonged to a Roman soldier called Longinus. Ever since then the Spear of Longinus (also known as the Holy Lance and the Spear of Destiny) has been regarded as a weapon of dark power. There have been several spears that have surfaced at various times in history, with claims made for them to be the Spear of Longinus. During World War II it is said that the Nazis were actively searching for the Spear, supposedly to harness its occult power.

The battles commence

The two brothers attacked the party of advancing knights and slew many, wounded a great many more and drove off the rest. King Ryan fought on with Balin, but was overcome by him.

"Spare me, I pray you," he called. "I am worth more to you alive than dead." And he agreed to give his allegiance to King Arthur, upon his honour as a knight.

Almost at the same time Merlin appeared at Camelot and informed Arthur of the great victory by Balin and Balan and the great service they had done him. Arthur then set out to deal with the other eleven kings whom King Ryan had forged to his will and who had no love of Arthur. They had now been joined by King Lot of Orkney who had always been Arthur's enemy and who hated him since he had been forced to give up Mordred, his son.

The battle took place at Castle Tarabil and it did not go well for Arthur's force. It seemed that he would lose until two knights entered the fray. These were Balin and Balan, both of whom fought so fiercely that the battle turned. By the end of the day, of the twelve kings only Lot remained alive. Then out of nowhere came King Pellinore. He fought with King Lot and dispatched him with a fearsome blow. He had proven Merlin's earlier prophesy.

Sir Balin and Sir Balan then took their leave of Arthur, much to his disappointment since they were such worthy and valiant knights, but Merlin had told him of Balin's quest and of their destiny. After this victory King Arthur led his army and went on to defeat the Saxons in six great battles.

The invisible knight and the Dolorous Stroke

After some days Balin had another adventure. A knight called Sir Garlon was able through magic to make himself invisible so that he could slay other knights in a most cowardly fashion. He was a member of King Pelles' entourage.

King Pelles held his court at Castle Carbonek and was due to hold a feast at which all knights were to attend with their ladies. Upon arrival they were to surrender their arms. This Balin did, but since he possessed two swords he kept the one that he had won from the Lady of the Lake secreted under his cloak and gave up the other. At the feast he had Sir Garlon pointed out to him and kept a close eye on him thereafter. Sir Garlon took exception to this scrutiny and insulted him, whereupon Balin stabbed him to prevent him using his power of invisibility to disappear and then kill him.

King Pelles regarded Sir Garlon as a brother and gave chase to Balin, determined to avenge Sir Garlon's death. They fought along the corridors and stairs until at last Balin's sword was broken in two. It

How Balin smote the Dolorous Stroke, by Alfred Kappes, 1881.

looked as if King Pelles would kill him but he ran into a room that seemed like a chapel. A cup lay on an altar and floating above it was a spear.

His mind in turmoil, he grabbed the spear and, despite the fact that King Pelles had dropped to his knees upon seeing the cup and the spear, he smote him a dreadful blow in the side, the Dolorous Stroke. Suddenly everything spun about Balin and he found himself diving into a pool of deep unconsciousness.

Merlin explains

It was three days before Balin regained consciousness, only to find himself lying in the ruins of the castle with many dead bodies around him. Unable to even move, it was not until Merlin came that he gained any true sense of what had happened.

Merlin took him away from the place and explained that the cup he had seen was the Holy Grail and the spear was the spear that had been used to wound Jesus Christ on the cross. The wound that he had given King Pelles would cause the King agony and would never heal until the

Holy Grail was found again and blood from the spear was administered by the good knight, Sir Galahad.

The act would also lay three countries to ruin and waste, and they would become known as the Waste Lands.

The prophesy comes true

Balin rode on towards his destiny with a heavy heart. At last he came to a castle and was greeted by the lady of the castle.

"Welcome, Sir Knight," she said. "Come, we will make you most welcome, but first it is the custom to joust with the Knight of the River."

The Knight of the River dwelled in the middle of the river and wore unmarked black armour. He soon came to meet Balin in combat, first on horse until each was flung from their mounts, and then on foot with drawn swords.

They were well matched and soon the ground about them was covered in blood. At last the Knight of the River collapsed from loss of blood and Sir Balin leaned on his sword. "What is your name, Sir Knight?" he asked.

The other threw back his helm and gasped, "I am Balan, brother of Sir Balin." And Balin, taking off his helm, knelt by his brother and wept, for neither had realised that their foe was their brother. And with many tears they both died.

The lady of the castle had them buried in the same tomb and had Sir Balin's name engraved on it. Then Merlin arrived and had Balan's name added and also, under Balin's name, the fact that he was the knight who had delivered the Dolorous Stroke.

As for the scabbard of the sword, Merlin left it near the island so that one day Galahad would find it. The sword he had put in a block of marble and then mystically suspended it above the water. One day in the future it would float down river to Camelot where it would present itself to Galahad, the good knight.

The Round Table

King Arthur respected Merlin's opinion and leaned heavily upon him for advice. After he had reigned for a while his nobles started to pressurise him to take a wife.

"How would you advise me?" he asked Merlin, for he did not wish to marry unless it was for love. As it happened, he was already in love with Princess Guinevere, daughter of King Leodegraunce, the ruler of Camelerd.

Merlin knew Arthur's nature and did not try to dissuade him, although

The Round Table.

he did advise him that marrying her could have consequences that he did not anticipate. He implied that a good knight and she might fall in love with each other and bring shame upon Camelot. In addition, he told him about the Holy Grail and the part that it would have to play in the future of his realm and in his life.

King Arthur then agreed for Merlin to visit King Leodegraunce and tell him of the king's love for his daughter. King Leodegraunce agreed willingly and arranged to come to Camelot at Pentecost, when his daughter would marry Arthur. As a dowry he presented King Arthur with a round table that had belonged to Uther Pendragon and which could seat one hundred and fifty knights. Since he accepted King Arthur's overall rule, he submitted one hundred of his own knights. Thus the Round Table came to Camelot.

King Arthur and Queen Guinevere

On the wedding morning during Pentecost several young men were knighted. These included Arthur's nephew, Gawain, King Lot's son, and Tor, King Pellinore's son. Then Arthur and Guinevere were married in the Church of Saint Stephen and all of the knights that were present pledged their allegiance to them both. All their subjects rejoiced at the union and wondered at the beauty of Queen Guinevere.

The wedding party filed into the banqueting hall where Merlin showed the assembled knights the Round Table with its one hundred and fifty sieges (seats), bidding them take the siege that had been allocated to them. A name appeared in letters of gold on the back of each siege to indicate which knight should sit there.

Thus was King Arthur's order of the Round Table established. Only the truest knights would be permitted to sit at the table. If one died or was slain then a new knight, if he was worthy and proved himself by carrying out some deed, would take his place.

"Yet there are still four places vacant," said King Arthur.

"One shall be given to King Pellinore of the Questing Beast," replied Merlin. "He will soon come to Camelot to rest from his quest. One will be taken by Sir Lancelot, the greatest living knight. Another will be taken by Sir Percival of Wales, who is not yet born. And the last seat shall be called the Siege Perilous. No-one may sit in it and live except for the knight who will come when the Holy Grail comes to Camelot. That knight will be the noblest and truest of all knights."

The knights all took their places but before the feast began, Merlin told them that they could expect to see a strange sight.

The first quest of the Round Table

No sooner had he said this than a white hart bounded into the hall pursued by a white bracket, or small hunting dog, then behind them a pack of black hounds. The hart ran round the table followed by the chasing animals. At the door the bracket almost caught the hart and snapped at it, but the hart leaped sidewards and knocked over a knight, who stood and snatched up the bracket and then strode out of the hall. He mounted his horse and rode out of Camelot with the bracket under his arm.

Then a damsel rode into the hall on a white palfrey, a great white horse with a magnificent saddle.

"King Arthur, help me, I pray. That knight has stolen my bracket."

But the king did not personally wish to be disturbed on his wedding day and told her that it was no affair of the Round Table. A fully armoured knight then rode into the hall and grabbed up the damsel and carried her off.

Merlin rebuked King Arthur for his reticence to help. "This is a quest such as you must take up for the honour of the Round Table."

And so King Arthur sent some of his knights on the quest:

- Sir Gawain to bring back the white hart
- Sir Tor to bring back the bracket
- King Pellinore to bring back the damsel and the knight who carried her off

Each of the knights had adventures.

Sir Gawain's adventure

The newly knighted Sir Gawain took his younger brother Gaheris with him as his squire. During his pursuit of the white hart he jousted with and defeated several knights, all of whom he sent back to Camelot to swear allegiance to King Arthur. At last he followed the hart into a castle and was horrified to see a knight setting about the hounds with his sword, slaying them all. Sir Gawain fought him and despite the fact that the knight asked for mercy, he was not prepared to be merciful. He was about to take his head off when the lady of the castle threw herself between them and Sir Gawain lopped off her head by accident.

He and Gaheris were captured by four knights but were set free by four ladies who told him that for penance he must return to Camelot bearing the lady's body and her head.

When he returned to Camelot and told the king and queen of his adventure he declared that for his shame at taking a lady's life, he would henceforth never refuse a damsel a request and would always show mercy to those who asked it.

Sir Tor's adventure

The other newly created knight, Sir Tor, followed the trail of the knight who took the bracket. He met two knights who challenged him. Sir Tor defeated them and, like Sir Gawain, sent them back to Camelot. Their servant, a dwarf, begged to accompany Sir Tor as his squire. The dwarf led him to a pavilion where three ladies were sleeping with the bracket beside one of them. Sir Tor crept away with it but woke one of the ladies who then told him that evil would befall him for stealing her bracket. He rode off but was soon pursued by the knight who took it from Camelot. They fought and Sir Tor vanquished him but the knight refused to yield, even though Sir Tor was loath to kill him. At that moment a lady came by on a palfrey and asked him to grant her a request as a knight of King Arthur's court. He granted the request, only to have her then say that she wanted the head of the knight because he had slain her brother.

The knight then begged for mercy but Sir Tor, having given the lady his word, avenged her brother's death. After staying with the lady and her husband, he and the dwarf returned to Camelot where he was given his seat at the Round Table.

King Pellinore's adventure

On leaving Camelot King Pellinore rode fast through the forest. By a well he saw a lady nursing a wounded knight who lay with his head in her lap. She asked Pellinore for help but he was in such haste that he rode on regardless. Unbeknown to him, the knight died and the lady was so distraught that she slayed herself with his sword.

King Pellinore tracked the knight who had taken the lady and found her safe in a pavilion guarded by two squires. Her name was Lady Viviene, sometimes known as the sorceress Nimue. When he asked her to go back to Camelot with him the squires told him that two knights were fighting for her nearby, and that he should stop them fighting and tell them that he was going to take the lady. He therefore rode off and found them on foot battling it out with swords. One of them was the lady's kinsman and he was trying to rescue her from the knight who took her from Camelot. Neither was willing to give up their claim on her and the evil knight slayed King Pellinore's horse so that he, too, would be on foot. Then both knights fought King Pellinore who overcame them and slayed the evil knight. The other craved mercy which Pellinore granted.

And so King Pellinore and the lady returned towards Camelot but on the way they came across the dead knight and the head of the lady who had been nursing him. Wild animals had devoured her body. With great sadness and guilt he took the knight's body to a hermitage to be buried and then bore the lady's head to Camelot.

He recounted his adventure to the king, queen and Merlin.

"Ah, King Pellinore, you were greatly to blame for the lady's death," said Queen Guinevere.

"Indeed," agreed Merlin. "Yet what you did not know is that the lady was Alyne, your own daughter. The knight was Sir Miles of Llandys, whom she was going to marry. He was a good and true knight. Because of this dark deed that has occurred it is decreed by fate that you shall be one day betrayed by the person that you trust more than any in the world."

Thus the first quest of the Round Table came to an end. King Arthur told his knights that henceforward his knights should uphold the laws of chivalry and of knighthood. As Knights of the Round Table, they had to swear:

- Always to give mercy when it was asked
- Always be true to their king and to Camelot
- Always aid ladies, damsels, gentlewomen and widows
- Never take advantage of women
- Never battle without just cause

Merlin's Fate

Despite all his wisdom and magic power, Merlin had foreseen that he would one day be buried alive. He had been completely captivated by the Lady Viviene, whom King Pellinore had rescued and brought back to Camelot. She was one of the ladies of the sacred Isle of Avalon.

King Arthur had leaned heavily upon Merlin's advice and had been dreading the time when he would leave him, as he had prophesied that he would some years before.

Merlin talked with Arthur one last time and warned him that Excalibur would be stolen by a woman that he had full trust in, and that he should be sure to keep the scabbard safe, for it gave him invulnerability. He also warned him that this evil woman would be related to the evil knight who would one day strike him down on the Field of Camlann. And yet, at the end she would prove to be a good woman who would care for him.

Viviene and Merlin, by Julia Margaret Cameron, albumen print, 1874.

Then Merlin left to woo the Lady Viviene and together they travelled widely. He taught her many spells and showed her many wonders. She made him promise never to take advantage of her either by force or by enchantment.

In France, they stayed and enjoyed the hospitality of King Pant and his wife Elaine. There they saw Elaine's son, who would become Sir Lancelot. And before he left Merlin prophesied to Queen Elaine that her son would one day become the greatest living knight and that one day he would have a son with another lady called Elaine. This child would become Sir Galahad, the greatest knight of them all.

Viviene greatly admired Merlin, yet she also feared the power of his magic. Unbeknown to him she had started looking for opportunities to trap him and prevent him from ever using his magic against her. Then she would become the most powerful wonder worker in the land.

At last, Viviene tricked Merlin into showing her a great wonder concealed under a great rock. When he had gone under it and descended a stairway to a great cavern she caused the rock to be sealed with Merlin trapped underneath for all eternity since he was unable, because of his promise, to use his magic to escape.

The battle with the five kings

King Arthur moved his court, as he was sometimes inclined to do, to Carlisle. While he was there he heard that five kings had invaded his lands. These were:

- The King of Denmark
- The King of Ireland
- The King of Vale

- The King of the Isle of Longtains
- The King of Sorleyse

"Alas," King Arthur moaned, "that I can never have a single month when I can rest from warring."

Sending word to King Pellinore to gather a force he, Guinevere and their force headed across country towards the River Humber where they set up camp. However, the five kings had travelled overnight and set upon Arthur's army while they slept. The army of the five kings pressed home their advantage and killed most of Arthur's men. King Arthur wished to fight, but he had his queen's safety in mind. So he, Guinevere and three knights – Sir Gawain, Sir Gryflet and Sir Kay – escaped and rode as fast as they could towards the river, meaning to find a way across it. They were pursued by the five kings alone, for they personally wished to finish Arthur.

Although there were five against four, the king and his three knights soon despatched the five kings. They put Queen Guinevere upon a barge on the river, then they returned to their camp where they found the survivors of their force.

On the following day, King Arthur, his three knights and the remnant of his army descended upon the leaderless army and killed thirty thousand of them. King Pellinore arrived with his force, too late for the battle but in time to praise King Arthur and his brave knights.

Morgan le Fay's evil plan

One day King Arthur was hunting in the forest with King Urien and Sir Accolon of Gaul and a party of others when they came upon and gave chase to a great white hart. They rode hard for several miles until their horses collapsed and died, whereupon they continued on foot, giving up the chase and

Morgan le Fay, by J.R. Spencer Stanhope, 1880.

focusing instead on finding lodgings for the night. Then they came upon the hart, which had been brought down by a pack of hounds close by the shore of a lake.

King Arthur raised his hunting horn to his lips to signal that a kill had been made. As the horn blast echoed across the waters a boat appeared from the mists upon the lake. Sensing the opportunity for an adventure, King Arthur suggested that they get on board the boat which duly sailed off.

It was an enchanted ship, luxuriantly furnished with silks and fine furniture. As night fell a hundred torches appeared and lit up the lake. And then twelve ladies appeared from nowhere and made the three knights welcome. They feasted and they drank and then all three fell asleep.

King Urien

King Urien awoke to find himself back in Camelot beside his wife, Morgan le Fay. She professed innocence, although she was behind the whole enterprise.

King Arthur

King Arthur awoke in a dungeon surrounded by many other knights who looked weak from lack of food or drink. They told him that they were in the castle belonging to Sir Damas, a false and base knight. While Sir Damas was a coward his brother Sir Outlake was brave and worthy, but having no lands or money he had challenged Sir Damas to single combat, the winner taking all the estate. Sir Damas knew that he would stand little chance against his brother so he sought a knight to act as his champion. However, since he was so hated he had been unable to get anyone to act as his champion. That was why he had captured all the knights who had passed nearby his castle on their various quests. He gave them a choice, to fight for him or to remain his prisoner forever. Thus far none had been prepared to fight for him.

King Arthur agreed to fight on condition that all of the prisoners be set free.

Sir Accolon

Sir Accolon awoke to find himself hanging on the side of a deep well, in danger of his life. A crystal fountain gushed water from a silver pipe. He crossed himself for he realised that the twelve ladies were fiends and that the ship had been enchanted.

A hideous dwarf appeared and told him that he came from Morgan le Fay. (He and she were actually lovers). The dwarf told Sir Accolon that he would be rescued if he would fight a knight in the morning. Morgan le Fay had arranged by magic for him to have both Excalibur and the magic scabbard so he would be sure to win. His rewards would be great.

And so it was arranged. Sir Damas released all his prisoners and had King Arthur arrayed in unmarked armour, with sword and lance. He sent word to his brother Sir Outlake to say that he had a champion who was ready to fight for him. This was not good news for Sir Outlake who had been wounded by a false knight and was in no condition to fight. Then by her magic Morgan le Fay arranged for Sir Accolon to be brought to his manor house where he agreed to fight as Sir Outlake's champion. Thus it was arranged that King Arthur and Sir Accolon would fight, neither knowing the identity of the other. But Sir Accolon had both the scabbard and Excalibur.

After taking mass, as was only fitting before such a battle, the two knights fought until the ground was thick with King Arthur's blood, for he could do nothing to wound Sir Accolon who was protected by the magic scabbard.

Yet Viviene had come to watch, for she suspected that Morgan le Fay had murderous plans for her half-brother. When Sir Accolon struck a mighty blow with Excalibur that broke Arthur's sword Viviene cast a spell that caused Excalibur to fall from Sir Accolon's hand. King Arthur immediately picked it up and grabbed the scabbard from his opponent's side and cast it away. Then he quickly overcame Sir Accolon, who refused to yield.

"Where are you from, Sir Knight?" Arthur asked.

"I am Sir Accolon of Gaul, from the court of King Arthur."

At that point, King Arthur removed his helm to reveal his identity and Sir Accolon confessed that he had been given the task of killing him so that he would become king. "This was promised me by Morgan le Fay."

Despite his treason, King Arthur spared him, for he had been a good knight. King Arthur then called Sir Damas and Sir Outlake to him, and for his sins he made Sir Damas pass all his estate to his brother and ordered him to make penance once a year. Then he ordered that he and Sir Accolon be taken to a nearby Abbey to have their wounds treated. It was, unfortunately, too late for Sir Accolon who died soon after from loss of blood.

Once his own wounds were healed King Arthur arranged for Sir Accolon's body to be taken back to Camelot and presented to Morgan le Fay, with the message that he once again had possession of Excalibur and the scabbard.

Morgan le Fay is denounced

King Arthur's half-sister was not aware that Arthur was still alive. She planned to kill her husband King Urien and put Sir Accolon on the throne beside her. She found her husband fast asleep in his chamber and ordered her maid to fetch his sword so that she could kill him in his sleep. The maid found Morgan le Fay's son, Sir Uwaine, asleep in a nearby chamber and told him of his mother's plan. He gave her the sword and told her to take it to her and he would deal with matters.

Queen Morgan le Fay prepared to slay her husband but just as she raised the sword Sir Uwaine rushed in and stayed her hand.

"You are a fiend!" he said. "I should by right strike off your head, for I have been born of a fiend."

The queen begged his forgiveness and claimed that she had been possessed by a malevolent spirit. Sir Uwaine forgave her and made her promise never to harbour such thoughts again.

Soon after, Sir Accolon's body was brought to Camelot and was laid in the church where Morgan le Fay saw it. Overcome with grief, if not with remorse, she determined to leave Camelot. Accordingly, she sought Queen Guinevere's permission to leave and straight away rode for the Abbey where King Arthur was staying. She was shown to his chamber and entered it alone, since none may refuse a queen. Inside she spied the King asleep with Excalibur at his side. Her plan was to once again steal the sword and scabbard.

"But if I wake him he will discover me and slay me," she mused to herself. With which she decided not to try to take Excalibur but to take the scabbard alone.

When King Arthur awoke he discovered the scabbard had been taken and he soon found out that Morgan le Fay, his half-sister, had been in his chamber. With Sir Outlake he set off in pursuit of her and her faithful knights. She, fearing that she could be caught, rode into a lake and threw the scabbard as far as she could so that it sank deep into the lake and could not be recovered. Then she and her followers rode on and eventually found themselves in a valley full of strangely shaped stones. Hearing King Arthur and Sir Outlake fast approaching, she used magic to turn herself and her knights into marble so that when the king arrived he was unable to find her or the missing scabbard.

A final message for King Arthur

Afterwards, as Queen Morgan le Fay and her party rode on they came upon a knight leading on horseback another knight who was blindfolded and bound hand and foot.

"Why is that knight bound?" she asked.

"He is a false knight who had been adulterous with my wife. I am going to drown him in the fountain and afterwards she will suffer the same fate."

"Is this true?" she asked the prisoner, who vigorously disagreed. When asked who he was he replied that he was Sir Manessen, a knight from the court of King Arthur and that he was a cousin to Sir Accolon of Gaul.

"It would be wrong to have such a thing happen," she said. "I deliver you and permit you to deal with your former captor however you will."

So she had him released and the other bound whereupon Sir Manessen duly drowned him in the fountain.

"Go now and tell King Arthur that I have rescued you, but that I did so for the sake of Sir Accolon and not because of the king. Tell him also that I do not fear him and that he will never find me, for I can turn myself and my knights into stone. He will understand."

And so saying she entered the country of Gore where she was well received and loved. There she strengthened her castles and towns for in her heart she did secretly dread the wrath of her brother, King Arthur.

Chapter Two

The Knights of the Round Table

In Arthur's dayes, whan he helde the Round Table moste plenoure, hit fortuned the kynge commaunded that the hyghe feste of Pentecoste sholde be holden at a cite and a castell...

Sir Gareth of Orkney, Le Morte d'Arthur,
Sir Thomas Malory

AFTER telling *The Tale of King Arthur* Sir Thomas Malory then goes on to recount several tales about King Arthur himself and his individual knights. Later in the book, when we look at the various sources, we shall see how deftly Malory wove the tales together into a continuous narrative. The middle part of his book is therefore

The Dedication, by John Pettie, 1884.

37

The Noble Tale of King Arthur who became Emperor of Rome

The main adventure that Malory describes is King Arthur's war with Rome, in which he defeats the Emperor Lucius and himself becomes emperor. This adventure is also described in the *Prose Merlin*, another work that dates back to the Thirteenth Century, so it predates Malory's book. Sir Gawain features prominently in this adventure.

---

predominantly about the adventures of the Knights of the Round Table, most of which have a good solid lesson to be learned from their actions, either positive or negative.

In this section we shall look at the adventures of some of the main characters who sat at the Round Table.

King Arthur's Adventures

Malory goes on to describe several of the King's adventures. The first, about how he became Emperor of Rome, is given a book to itself. Others are mere preface adventures to the great tales of his Knights of the Round Table.

King Arthur and the Great Cat of Lausanne

This adventure also comes from *Prose Merlin*. Merlin and Sir Gawain join the king in this adventure. It takes place in the land of Lausanne (Switzerland) where a demon in the form of a great cat is terrorising the people, killing and devouring at will.

A fisherman had gone fishing for something to give to the Lord, but after catching several fish of increasing size which he kept for himself he finally caught a small kitten. This he took home to catch rats and mice but it grew up to be a monster, eventually strangling both the fisherman and his wife before becoming completely feral and out of control. It made its home in a cave on a mountain overlooking the Lake of Lausanne.

Merlin showed Arthur the cave in which the cat lived, then retreated as the king did battle with it. Both Arthur and the cat suffered grievous wounds but ultimately Arthur killed it after cutting off its legs, while leaving its feet buried deeply in his shield.

After showing the body of the beast to the people to reassure them, Arthur had it buried with honour. Ever afterwards, the mountain was called the Mountain of the Cat.

The Giant of St Michael's Mount

This great Cornish landmark was in days gone by said to have been built by a giant called Cormoran who would wade ashore from the Mount and capture stray sheep, cows or wayfarers and take them back to his castle to eat. Local legends link it with the British fairy tale about Jack the Giant Killer, a young boy who rows out one night, digs a trap and then blows a horn to get the giant to fall into the hole and break his neck.

In this adventure King Arthur is aided by Sir Kay and Sir Bedivere, yet it is he who fights with the giant, first blinding him in one eye and then defeating him by guile. The giant catches him, but since he cannot see, he is fooled when Arthur throws down his sword onto rocks so that it makes a great noise. The giant immediately gropes for it, not expecting the king to have disarmed him. As he does, Arthur knees him under the chin, knocking him unconscious. He then orders Sir Bedivere to cut off Cormoran's head and tie it to his horse so that it can be shown to the people.

Sir Gawain and the Green Knight

This is actually a tale that Malory missed out; it may be that he was not aware of it. Later in the book we shall look at some of the sources that Sir Thomas Malory used in compiling his great work. One source that he did not use was that of the Pearl Poet, or the Gawain Poet, as the elusive author of the adventure of *Sir Gawain and the Green Knight* is known.

Other authors, including Roger Lancelyn Green, did include this medieval tale, which seems entirely appropriate since it starts in

King Arthur's court at Camelot and involves Sir Gawain, one of the greatest and worthiest knights. We have followed suit and place it here at the start of the adventures of the Knights of the Round Table.

Sir Gawain and the Green Knight, medieval illumination by unknown artist.

A test of valour

One year at Christmas King Arthur was holding his regular feast at Camelot. All the knights were present and Queen Guinevere was sitting under a great embroidered canopy. As was customary by this time, the feast could not begin until some quests were presented to the Round Table.

Suddenly there was a great tumult and a terrible figure on horseback rode into the hall. It was a giant of a knight, clad completely in green, with green skin, a great green beard and a mane of green hair. Even his horse was green. He carried no shield or weapons other than a huge axe of green steel.

King Arthur bid him welcome and invited him to join their feast but the Green Knight replied that he was not there for feasting, but to see whether the rumours were true, that at the court of King Arthur there were brave and worthy knights. King Arthur replied that if battle or jousting were what he sought then there were many knights who would meet him in combat. At this the Green Knight laughed and taunted them for being unworthy and not brave enough. Besides, he told them, he had come to offer a test of valour to any one person among them who was prepared to exchange stroke for stroke with him, using his axe.

"I will stand here and receive a single stroke from him, on any part of the body he wishes. They for their honour must then receive a similar stroke from me twelve months hence."

King Arthur was infuriated by this and rose to take up the challenge himself. Yet Sir Gawain, his nephew, who had only recently been knighted, sensed the danger to his uncle, for it would be a mortal challenge. Perceiving how awful it would be for Guinevere to have to live a year with such an awful fate awaiting her husband, he accepted the challenge and took the axe from the Green Knight.

The giant knight stood his ground and awaited Sir Gawain's blow. When it came it was a mighty blow which severed the head from the body in a gush of blood. Yet the Green Knight did not fall. He walked to his severed head and picked it up by the long green hair, collected his axe from the dumb-struck Gawain and mounted his horse.

"Upon your honour," the decapitated head cried out. "In twelve months' time, on this day, meet me at the Green Chapel in the north of the country and be prepared to accept my blow in return."

He galloped from the hall leaving everyone speechless and Gawain realising that he may have only a year left to live.

Sir Gawain at Christmas

The year passed and at the feast of Michaelmas King Arthur and his court prepared to bid farewell to Gawain, for he had to find his way to the Green Chapel which was somewhere in the north, possibly in Wales.

So off he rode on his mighty steed Gringalet, braving foes and whatever hardship the elements threw at him. Everywhere he went he asked if people had heard of the Green Knight or of the Green Chapel.

At last, as Christmas approached Sir Gawain hoped and prayed to find somewhere where he might take mass. Almost mystically, he came upon a great castle and was admitted and made most welcome by the lord of the castle and his lady, for his renown as a Knight of the Round Table had preceded him. He and the knight, whose name was Sir Bertilak de Hautdesert, the Knight of the Lake, became close friends and Gawain was invited to stay over the Christmas period. Gawain thanked him but said that he could not stay, for he was on a quest and must present himself at the Green Chapel on New Year's Day. Sir Bertilak told him not to worry because the Green Chapel was a mere two miles away so he could stay and be merry and enjoy their hospitality.

The lady of the castle was a beauty and she was clearly smitten by Sir Gawain. There was also an ancient lady of noble birth who resided in the castle. She befriended Gawain who was ever courteous to her, not realising that she was Morgan le Fay, King Arthur's half-sister and a powerful sorceress.

The lord of the castle proposed a contract. He would go hunting and give Gawain whatever he hunted and killed and in return Gawain would give him whatever he gained while staying in the castle. Over three days the lord went hunting, and on each of those days his wife attempted to seduce Gawain.

Exchanging gifts

On the first day Sir Bertilak hunted and killed a hart. The lady gave Gawain a single kiss, so when Sir Bertilak gave him the hart, he gave a kiss. He honourably refused to say from whence he won the kiss.

On the second day Sir Bertliak killed a wild boar. The lady gave Gawain two kisses and he in turn kissed Sir Bertilak twice.

On the third day, Sir Bertilak killed a fox. Yet again Sir Gawain adroitly turned down Lady Bertilak's seduction attempts although on this occasion his resolve had weakened. She wanted to give him a gold ring but he refused. Instead he agreed to accept a green girdle that she said had been woven with magic to protect its wearer from physical harm. He accepted this and agreed not to tell her husband about it. She bestowed three kisses upon him, which he then gave to Sir Bertilak when he accepted the fox fur.

At the Green Chapel

On New Year's Day Sir Gawain made ready. He clothed and armoured himself, tying the green girdle about himself, noting that it looked quite inconspicuous. He then took his leave of his hosts and was guided to the Green Chapel by a servant. This servant took him directly there, telling him frightening tales about the Green Knight which undoubtedly heightened Gawain's state of unease at the prospect ahead.

The Green Chapel was reached by passing through a valley and entering a chasm. It was a natural cathedral, overgrown with greenery. As Gawain approached he heard the grinding of an axe. He called out and was told to wait, for he was bound by his vow, and in any case the strike would come soon enough.

Gawain endeavoured to stand his ground and show no fear as the Green Knight approached. He bared his neck and awaited the strike.

As the Green Knight raised his axe, Gawain flinched involuntarily. The Green Knight then chided him for being cowardly, prompting Gawain to hold himself firm. 'Then strike, for I will not flinch again.'

The Green Knight swung the axe again and this time stayed its descent a fraction of an inch from Sir Gawain's neck.

'Ah, so you have your courage back,' he cried. 'Then I can truly strike a brave man, as was the challenge I gave.'

And on the third occasion he swung the axe, causing it to slice a deep cut on Gawain's neck, but nothing more.

Blood splattered on the stone but realising that he was still alive and now freed from his vow, Gawain pulled on his helmet and with his sword prepared to fight.

The Green Knight then raised a hand and said that there was no need, for he had proven himself a good and worthy knight. Then he revealed that he was well aware of what had been happening while he was away hunting.

"The first and second blows were for promises truthfully kept, since you received kisses from my wife and gave them to me. The third blow was for a promise only half kept, since you gave me three kisses yet kept that green girdle which belongs to me."

Realising that the Green Knight was his host Sir Bertilak changed by magic, Gawain felt that he had disgraced his knighthood by being untrue. Sir Bertilak remonstrated and told him that it was in the scheme of things a minor indiscretion, yet one which had been dealt with by the receipt of this minor wound. He bore no ill feeling and told him how it had all been contrived between him and his wife, at the instigation of Morgan le Fay, who had wished to test King Arthur and the Knights of the Round Table, and frighten Queen Guinevere, perhaps so much that she would die.

He asked Gawain to return with him to celebrate the New Year but Gawain refused. He felt that he should return to Camelot. He offered to return the green girdle, but Sir Bertilak told him to wear it with honour. As friends they parted.

King Arthur, Queen Guinevere and the court were delighted to receive Gawain back again. He recounted his adventure and denounced himself for being untrue. Yet no-one agreed and King Arthur felt that he should always wear the green girdle. Indeed, he said that henceforward all the Knights of the Round Table would wear a green sash in honour of Sir Gawain and the principles of knighthood that he had upheld so well.

Sir Lancelot Du Lac

Sir Lancelot is one of the most famous Knights of the Round Table. He is also extremely important to the overall legend as recounted by Sir Thomas Malory, for he should have been the greatest and worthiest knight of all. He is actually not mentioned in some of the earliest sources but is introduced by Chrétien de Troyes in the Twelfth Century.

The following is his first great adventure, although as the reader will see, he clearly had already established a considerable reputation as a champion.

While Sir Lancelot was sleeping

One year before the feast of Pentecost King Arthur and some of his knights went hunting in the forests outside Camelot. Soon they came upon a wounded knight being carried in a litter by four squires. He had a grievous head wound and was being carried to Camelot, for he believed that only there could his wound be healed by the truest and most worthy of knights. A shard of sword blade was still in the wound.

On the day of the feast of Pentecost three young knights were admitted to the fellowship of the Round Table. They were:

King Arthur and Sir Lancelot, by William Morris, 1862.

- Sir Lancelot of the Lake
- Sir Lionel, his cousin
- Sir Hector de Maris, half-brother of Sir Lancelot

The wounded knight was brought into the great hall. All of the knights were invited by King Arthur to lay hands on the wound to try and heal it. None was able to affect it, but at Sir Lancelot's touch the metal shard came free and the wound began to heal.

Some days later Sir Lancelot and his cousin Sir Lionel set out hoping to find their first adventure. After riding for several hours Sir Lancelot felt excessively sleepy and so the two knights dismounted. Lancelot removed his helmet and fell asleep under an apple tree beside a spring.

While he slept, Sir Lionel saw three knights riding fast through the forest pursued by a huge knight. This knight struck them down, one by one. Then he threw each across his own horse and rode off.

"I can achieve honour here," said Sir Lionel to himself. So saying, he mounted, leaving his cousin to sleep and set off in pursuit of the knight. In a clearing he haled him and challenged him to fight. The knight accepted the challenge; the two rode against each other with lances in place, and Sir Lionel was unhorsed. Then, before he could do anything about it, he was bound, thrown over his horse and taken away with the other knights. They were taken to a castle where the large knight removed their armour and beat them with thorns before casting them into a dark, deep dungeon in which several other knights were already held prisoner. They had all been beaten by the large knight, whose name was Sir Tarquyn. Seemingly, he was a knight who hated the fellowship of the Round Table.

Meanwhile Sir Hector de Maris had missed his half-brother and cousin and rode out of Camelot in the hope of meeting them or of finding adventure of his own. In the forest he asked a woodsman if he knew where he might find adventure. He was directed to a castle where he would find a tree upon which hung the shields of knights who Sir Tarquyn had either slain or overcome and captured. Sir Hector was angered when he saw the shield of Sir Lionel, so he struck a copper gong to induce the owner of the castle to come and joust with him.

Sir Tarquyn duly came and they broke a lance on each other's shield, before Sir Hector was defeated. His life was spared because he was a good fighter, yet he was given the same treatment as all the others and was cast into the dungeon.

The Nameless Knight

Through it all, Sir Lancelot still slept, blissfully unaware of the fate of his comrades. While he slept, four queens came along through the forest, riding upon four white mules, shielded from the sun by a canopy held at each corner by a mounted knight carrying a long spear. They were enchantresses and one of them was Morgan le Fay, King Arthur's half-sister. They ordered that the sleeping Sir Lancelot should be carried back to Castle Charyot, Morgan le Fay's castle, where he was unclad and left in a dungeon.

"He will sleep under this enchantment, for it was indeed an enchanted sleep, for another seven hours. When he awakes, he will be given a choice – choose one of us, or die."

When he awoke Sir Lancelot was confronted by the four queens:

- Morgan le Fay, Queen of Gore
- The Queen of North Gaul
- The Queen of Estlond
- The Queen of the Outer Isles

Morgan le Fay told him that he must choose one of them but he replied that according to his honour he could not. He knew that they were enchantresses, and that if he had his liberty he would choose one such as Queen Guinevere. He was therefore left to consider his fate while they considered the manner of his death.

He was brought food and drink by a damsel, who told him that she was the daughter of King Bagdemagus and that if he would fight on her father's behalf at the forthcoming tournament she would help him to escape.

Two days later Sir Lancelot appeared at the tournament on King Bagdemagus' behalf as the Nameless Knight, using borrowed armour with neither device nor distinguishing feature. His vanquished foes were instructed to present themselves to King Arthur at Camelot and say that they were defeated by the Nameless Knight.

Sir Lancelot then rode away and a couple of days later came across a joust between two knights. One was Sir Gaheris, the brother of Sir Gawain and the other was Sir Tarquyn. Sir Gaheris was defeated and as was Sir Tarquyn's way he was thrown across his horse and driven towards his castle. Sir Lancelot then challenged Sir Tarquyn to combat and they fought long and hard.

"You are the mightiest knight that I have ever come across," Sir Tarquyn said, as they leaned on their swords, recovering breath and regaining their strength, for the ground by then was covered in blood from their many wounds. "I love a good warrior and to show my love for you I will release all of my prisoners, just as long as you are not one knight. That knight is Lancelot, who slew my brother Sir Carados of the Dolorous Tower."

"Then fight on," replied Lancelot, "for it is I who slew your brother, an evil and craven knight."

The fight continued until Sir Lancelot beheaded the huge knight. He released Sir Gaheris, who was also wounded, and told him to go and release their fellows. This Gaheris did, explaining to all what had happened, including Sir Kay, a knight who had been scathing about Sir Lancelot when he had first seen him. He also informed them that Sir Lancelot would meet them all at the next Pentecost.

Sir Lancelot found that his wounds were not too bad and went off in search of further adventures.

The Tale of Sir Gareth of Orkney

This tale is typical in that it describes the deeply held concept of honour that a knight should have. Lord Tennyson writes of this tale in his poem *Gareth and Lynette*. Once again, it begins at the feast of Pentecost when the Round Table assembles and King Arthur refuses to eat until an adventure or a quest presents itself.

King Arthur clapped his hands and called out, "Let the feast begin, for here comes a young man dressed in simple attire."

Soon, a fair young man came into the hall and knelt before King Arthur.

Sir Gareth Beaumain of the Round Table battling the evil Red Knight, by Arthur Rackham.

47

"If it please you, most noble King Arthur, I have come to ask for three gifts. None of them amount to much, nor would any of them be difficult to give, or cause any pain in the giving. I would ask only one now and the others twelve months from now."

King Arthur was intrigued and bid him continue, for he was minded to grant the three gifts.

"First, my Lord, I ask that I may have food and drink at your court for a year." The king agreed and asked his name. The young man asked that he may give his name when the time was right. King Arthur then gave Sir Kay the task of looking after him and ensuring that he had food and drink.

Sir Kay did so reluctantly, expressing his view that the young man was a wastrel who only wanted to be kept at the king's expense and that after a year of eating pies in the castle kitchens he would simply be a fat, useless oaf. He called him Beaumains, meaning fair hands, for he had never seen anyone with such large, fair hands.

After a year the young man came again to King Arthur and Queen Guinevere on the feast of Pentecost. He was neither fat nor useless as Sir Kay had predicted. The court did not sit down to feast, for as usual they awaited some adventure to come. It came in the form of a damsel called Lady Lynette who knelt and begged the king for help.

"My sister, The Lady Lyones, is being held captive by the Knight of the Red Lands."

At this Beaumains came forward and knelt before the king and queen, reminding them of the two gifts he had yet to ask for. First he asked to be granted the adventure that the lady had just introduced. Secondly, he asked that Sir Lancelot should accompany him and if he proved worthy, to be knighted by him.

Lady Lynette was angered by this, for she had come to Camelot to ask for a knight, not a low born kitchen boy, to help her. She mounted her palfrey and rode off in an ill temper.

Beaumains readied himself and left the hall. A great steed awaited him with a dwarf, who presented him with a sword. He rode off after Lady Lynette and a short while after, Sir Lancelot followed.

Sir Kay was angry at this display by his kitchen boy, Beaumains, and he mounted his charger and rode after them, meaning to castigate and chastise the youngster. Shortly afterwards he caught up with him and shouted abuse, asking if he did not know him. Beaumains replied that he did indeed know him and that he was the rudest and most ungentle of knights. Sir Kay then charged at him with his spear at the ready, despite the fact that Beaumains was not armoured. Yet Beaumains skilfully used his sword and unhorsed the knight. Sir Lancelot arrived and despatched Sir Kay back to Camelot on his horse. Then he followed again.

The Lady Lynette was rude to Beaumains, cursing him for his low birth and his lack of skill. She supposed that he would prove himself to be a coward when he met the Knight of the Red Lands. Yet he was anything but cowardly, beating in succession a number of knights, each of whom was backed up by fellow-knights:

- Sir Perarde, the Knight of the Black Lands
- Sir Pertolope, the Knight of the Green Lands
- Sir Perymones, the Knight of the Blue Lands
- Sir Ironside, the Knight of the Red Lands

Beaumains' identity revealed

After defeating this last knight, Beaumains was knighted by Sir Lancelot. He then told Lancelot that his true identity was Gareth, son of King Lot of Orkney and Queen Morgawse, and younger brother of Gawain, Gaheris and Agravaine. He was half-brother to Mordred.

Gareth defeated Sir Ironside, the knight of the Red Lands, who had the strength of seven knights. This knight confessed that he was only fighting and killing knights because he was in love with a lady who desired the death of Sir Lancelot. Ultimately, he would come to him and be killed – yet Sir Gareth had defeated him. Sir Gareth spared him and sent him, as he had sent the others he had defeated, to pay allegiance to King Arthur. He then rode on to Castle Dangerous to rescue the Lady Lyones and seek her love. Yet when he rode up to the castle she spied him and insulted him as being unworthy. He rode off in broken spirits. The Lady Lynette, then seeing that Gareth was a true knight, angrily told her sister what a fine knight he was. She had been ever fearful for him, hence her behaviour towards him.

There are two ending to this tale:

- According to Malory, Gareth and Lady Lyones eventually fall in love and marry, once she is sure that he is of noble blood. Lady Lynette marries his brother, Sir Gaheris
- According to Tennyson, more satisfyingly perhaps, Lady Lynette nurses Sir Gareth of his wounds and declares her love for him and they marry

Sir Tristram and Isolde

Here we have one of the great medieval romances. It is a tale of courtly love that Tennyson delighted in.

Malory starts by acknowledging that King Arthur was overlord of the kingdoms of Wales, Ireland and Scotland and of many other realms all the way to Rome. Wales had two kings, Cornwall and Lyoness in the west had two kings, Ireland had 'two or three' and France had one, as did Bretayne.

The two kings of Cornwall in the west that he referred to were King Mark of Cornwall and King Meliodas of Lyoness. King Meliodas was the father of Tristram.

Lost Lyoness

Lyoness was a land said to border Cornwall but which is no more. Some say, fancifully perhaps, that it may have been the site of the final great battle where Arthur would perish. It was said to have fallen into the sea after the days of Arthur. It is possibly somewhere around the Scilly Isles.

King Arthur heard from Sir Lancelot of a noble knight of Lyoness and wanted to invite him to Camelot, for he sounded as if he might be a worthy addition to the fellowship of the Round Table. His name was Tristram, which meant sorrow, for his mother Queen Elizabeth, who was the sister of King Mark of Cornwall, had died giving birth to him. His father, King Meliodas, grieved for her for several years and then married again. His new wife was the daughter of King Howellis of Bretayne and they had a son. The new queen worried that her son would never inherit Lyoness, so she tried to poison Tristram. Unfortunately, her own son drank the poisoned drink and died. This made her more determined than ever to poison Tristram and she tried again, but this time King Meliodas picked up the poisoned goblet and was about to drink from it when she dashed it from his hand. Realising that the goblet must be poisoned, he made her confess. This treasonable act meant that she would be burned at the stake. Tristram begged his father to let her live, for he had forgiven her despite knowing that she had tried to kill him.

King Meliodas worried for his son so he sent him away, to be tutored in French, harp playing and other accomplishments by a faithful servant called Governal. He grew up to be an honourable man and a great knight.

After several years Tristram went to Cornwall and became the champion of his uncle, King Mark. Soon after, King Angwish of Ireland sent a messenger to say that Cornwall owed him tribute and that it must be sent. King Mark refused but said that he could send a champion to meet King Angwish's champion in battle.

Sir Morholt, the Irish champion, was the brother of the Queen of Ireland. He came and fought Tristram on the Isle of Samson. Tristram injured him with a mighty blow to the head, which left a fragment of his sword in the wound. He was taken home to Ireland, where despite the ministrations of his sister he died. She removed the shard of metal from the sword and kept it in a casket.

Tristram fell ill, for he had been wounded by poison on Sir Morholt's spear. King Mark sent him to Ireland where he purported to be a minstrel and was healed by the Princess Isolde. His sword was seen, however,

The fight between Tristram and Sir Marhaus, stained glass, by Dante Gabriel Rossetti, 1862–3.

51

and the missing piece matched the shard that the queen held in her casket. As a result, he was forced to leave the country.

When he returned to King Mark he described the beautiful Isolde and his uncle fell in love with the description. He again despatched Tristram to Ireland to woo her on his behalf. Isolde agreed to the union, although she had feelings for Tristram. On the boat back to Cornwall Tristram and Isolde inadvertently drank a love potion that her mother had intended Isolde and King Mark to drink. Thereafter they became bound in love forever.

Isolde married King Mark but the feelings of the two young people were too powerful for them. They became lovers and King Mark became suspicious. They therefore ran away together to live in the forest. Yet King Mark wanted her back and agreed to take her as long as Tristram was never to return and never to see her again.

Thus, Tristram went to the court of King Arthur where he became one of the greatest of the Knights of the Round Table. After some time, he went to Bretayne where he married another Isolde, known as Isolde the White. Yet he was in love with her name rather than the woman and he never consummated the marriage.

In another fight he was again wounded by a poisoned weapon and sent word for Isolde of Ireland to come to heal him if she would. A signal had been arranged. If Isolde was going to come then the ship returning would have a white sail but if she refused, it would be black. Isolde the White learned of this and when the ship was sighted and Tristram asked her the colour of its sail, she replied that it was black. In total despair, Tristram died. Then when Isolde arrived and found that he had died she killed herself.

Realising how much they had loved each other, Isolde the White was full of remorse.

Sir Tristram and la Belle Ysoude, stained glass, 1862–63.

Sir Percival

Malory introduces Sir Percival as a fully fledged knight. Yet other tales describe his early life. This is fairly important, since he becomes one of the three Grail Knights who play such a significant part in the Quest for the Holy Grail. The tale also helps to describe his youthful and innocent approach to life.

Percival and the Red Knight

In the wilds of Wales the widow of a good knight lived alone with her son, Percival, in a cave. He grew to be a strong and resourceful youth, skilled with a dart and fleet of foot. Yet since he had never met anyone else in his first fifteen years, he was unaware of the wickedness in the world. He was simple, honest and true.

One day he met a knight, who happened to be Sir Lancelot. There and then he decided that he would like to be a knight one day.

"How may I become a knight, such as you?" he asked. Lancelot told him that if he truly wished it then he had simply to go to the court of King Arthur and ask if he could become one. He was to tell him that he had been sent by Lancelot. The king would send him on deeds to prove his worth, and if found worthy he would be knighted. Yet he told him also that the most important thing was not prowess in arms, but to remain pure and humble in heart and to do things in the name of God.

Percival discussed this with his mother who reluctantly agreed that it was time for him to seek his way in the world. She advised him always to be true and honourable, as was his father. He must never take a kiss from a girl, except with a ring. Percival set off the following day, clad in goatskins and with his dart.

Later that day he came to a glade in the forest where a pavilion had been set up. Inside was a sleeping maiden, so beautiful that he desired to kiss her. Yet he remembered his mother's advice and exchanged her ring for his own. Then he kissed her gently and left, in love with her.

King Arthur's court had moved to Caerleon for Easter, as was the king's pleasure when travelling his realm. Percival arrived and peered into the Great Hall where King Arthur, Queen Guinevere and the knights were about to enjoy a feast. Sir Kay had a golden goblet full of wine that he was about to present to the king, and which would then be handed around the assembly. Suddenly a knight entered clad in a suit of red armour. He chided the fellowship, grabbed the goblet and drained it. Then he left carrying the goblet.

King Arthur was incensed and asked who would go and retrieve the goblet from the thief. Many knights offered to go but King Arthur said that it was a task beneath that of a knight, but that a squire desiring to show his worth should go. At this, Percival entered, knelt and begged to be given the task.

Sir Kay was scornful for he saw nothing but a goatherd boy. King Arthur disagreed, for he saw something in the lad and asked his name. Percival answered him and the king gave him the quest. So, furnished with a horse he left, and caught up with the Red Knight. Although he had no armour, yet he challenged the Red Knight who attacked him with his spear. Percival was nimble and used his dart to good effect, unhorsing the Red Knight who fell and broke his neck. Percival then tried unsuccessfully to remove the Red Knight's armour, which he needed if he was to become a knight. An elderly knight named Sir Gonemans rode by and showed him how to remove armour and how to put it on.

Percival stayed with Sir Gonemans over many months and learned much from him about art, courtly behaviour, fighting with weapons and about the ways of knighthood. Percival's simple upbringing without guile was a sound basis for learning about the higher purpose of knighthood.

Percival and Blanchefleur

One day Percival rode away in search of adventure and came across a mystical castle. He entered and found a magical chessboard which played by itself. He was about to tamper with the pieces when a damsel appeared and stopped him. It was Blanchefleur, the beautiful girl that he had kissed and whose ring he wore. Both of them had been unable to stop thinking of the other, even though she had only seen him in her dreams.

Then there was a peel of thunder and three mysterious women entered, one carrying the Holy Grail, another carrying a salver and the third a spear. Percival and Lady Blanchefleur bowed as they passed. She told him that this was the Grail Procession and that soon it would be coming to Logres. Yet Sir Lancelot would have to come and see it, and then one day it would come to Camelot and would appear there. Yet that would only happen when Sir Galahad sat in the Siege Perilous. She told him that it was his destiny to be one of the Grail Knights, but that now he must return to King Arthur's court.

On his way to the court he was met by four knights: Sir Kay, Sir Gawain, Sir Ywain and King Arthur himself. Sir Kay challenged him and was unhorsed by Percival. Then, realising who he was and that he had defeated the Red Knight, he was knighted and given his place at the Round Table next to Sir Gawain and the Siege Perilous.

He had many other adventures but his main quest was to find Blanchefleur and Carbonek in the Quest for the Holy Grail.

Sir Lancelot and Elaine

After the great battle of Mount Badon there were many years of peace in the realm. For many of the Knights of the Round Table it was a time of reflection and contemplation. Sir Lancelot – who had been in love with Queen Guinevere for many years but had never spoken of his feelings – led a tormented life. He loved yet could not express his love, for he held King Arthur in such high esteem and was loyal to the fellowship of the Round Table.

One Easter a hermit came to Camelot. He was made welcome and he talked with King Arthur and the knights. He told them that the Siege Perilous would one day be filled but the knight who would occupy it was not yet born. He would be the one who would achieve the Quest for the Holy Grail.

Then he told them the reason why he had come. It was to seek help from the greatest of their knights, to save a lady who was being kept by enchantment at the Dolorous Tower.

Sir Lancelot was given the task and he rode with the hermit across the land until he arrived at the Dolorous Tower, wherein the enchantress Morgan le Fay had imprisoned the damsel. She lay in a tub of boiling water. The enchantment was broken by Sir Lancelot's worthiness and the Dolorous lady was released.

The hermit then asked him to release the neighbouring district from the terror of a dragon that lived in a cromlech, (a megalithic chamber tomb). This he did and then he rode into the surrounding wasteland.

Soon he came to a mysterious castle that lay in ruins. This was Carbonek, the castle of King Pelles, the Fisher King.

When Sir Lancelot entered he saw the king lying on a couch with his knights sitting around him. He explained that he was Pelles, the King of the Waste Lands and of Haunted Carbonek. He was lame from a wound and could not walk.

There was a clap of thunder and the Grail Procession appeared. Sir Lancelot asked its meaning and King Pelles explained that he was a descendant of Joseph of Arimathea who held the sacred trust to look after the Holy Grail. The procession consisted of the Holy Grail (the cup that Jesus drank from at the last supper), the salver from which he ate and the spear that was used on him upon the cross. The Holy Grail was also used to catch his blood.

Elaine in the Barge, by Lancelot Speed, 1919.

Sir Lancelot stayed many days with King Pelles but they spoke no more of the Holy Grail and it was not seen again.

King Pelles had a daughter called Elaine who had fallen in love with Sir Lancelot, yet her love was unrequited. At last, in a desperate attempt to gain him she sought the help of Brysen, her maid, who was an enchantress almost as skilled in her craft as Morgan le Fay. She told Elaine that Lancelot loved only Queen Guinevere and she devised a plan.

A man came one day bearing a ring belonging to Queen Guinevere with the message that Sir Lancelot should go to her at Case Castle. There, he found Elaine

56

disguised by enchantment as Queen Guinevere. They slept together and she conceived a child.

Sir Lancelot was distraught when he awoke to find that he had slept with Elaine. He felt that he had betrayed his king, his vows and the fellowship of the Round Table. Angry at Elaine's deceit, he went quite mad and left the castle to wander in the Waste Lands for many months. Meanwhile, Elaine gave birth to Galahad.

Eventually, Sir Lancelot was found by Lady Elaine and Brysen by a well. They told King Pelles who ordered that no-one should try to rouse him, but that he should be placed in the tower wherein the Holy Grail was kept. A holy man revealed the Grail and its presence cured Lancelot who then returned to Camelot. Galahad was given into the care of holy monks who brought him up.

Lady Elaine fell into a deep sorrow at the loss of Lancelot and was wracked with guilt at having deceived him. She died and was placed in a great barge which was later found floating down the river to Camelot. A letter written to Sir Lancelot told of her woe and her love for him.

She was buried with great honour in the minster at Winchester. Sir Lancelot carried the stain on his honour for the rest of his life, yet all the time his love for Queen Guinevere grew stronger. It was that forbidden love which would bring about the fall of Camelot. But first would come the Quest for the Holy Grail.

The Fisher King

This character appeared in many myths and legends. He was a king wounded by the Dolorous Stroke, either from the spear of Longinus or from the Dolorous Sword. The wound could not be healed by ordinary methods, indeed it would only be healed by the blood of Christ given by the Grail Knight.

Very significantly, the Dolorous Stroke resulted in three lands being laid to waste, hence the Waste Lands. They too could only be restored by the blood of Christ and the Coming of the Holy Grail. This is the whole purpose of the Tale of the Holy Grail.

Geraint and Enid

An oft-told tale

This is a great tale told in *The Mabinogian* and by Tennyson, as well as in Chrétien de Troyes' version as *Erec et Enide*. The tale starts at Easter, at Caerleon, where King Arthur had moved his court for the feast.

A tall, handsome young squire called Geraint, son of Erbin, came to the court with news that he had seen a pure white stag with golden horns. King Arthur thanked him for his news and arranged to go off on a hunt for it the next day. He told Geraint that he should have its head, provided that he gave it to his true love. Geraint replied that he had no lady since he was simply an untried squire, but he hoped to be a knight. Queen Guinevere laughed and said that she would find him a lady, and that on the morrow she and her lady would accompany him on the hunt.

They set off after the king and his knights and on the way they saw a huge knight in black armour upon a huge black horse, accompanying a fair lady along the road. The queen was curious as to their identity and so her lady asked a dwarf who was accompanying them.

"That you may not know, because you are not worthy," replied the dwarf. And when she tried to pass him to ask the knight herself he lashed her across the face with his whip.

The lady was distraught and returned to the queen who was outraged. She then sent Geraint who received similar treatment. Geraint curbed his temper for killing the dwarf would serve no purpose, and he had no armour so would be no match for an armoured knight. He offered to follow them while the queen and her lady returned to Caerleon.

"Perhaps along the way I will be able to borrow armour from someone and challenge the Black Knight."

"Do so," Queen Guinevere agreed, "and when you return you shall be a Knight of the Round Table."

Geraint followed across hill and dale, through forests, valleys and alongside rivers until they came to a town and passed through to enter a mighty castle. The townspeople bowed and welcomed the Black Knight but gave Geraint not so much as a friendly smile. He rode on through the town and came to a once prosperous manor house surrounded by a stagnant moat. An old man in worn clothes greeted him and offered him shelter. His name was Liconal and he was the former duke of the surrounding country.

They enjoyed a frugal meal in the ruined hall. The duke's wife, an old lady and their daughter, a beautiful maid called Enid, ate with them. Liconal explained that the Black Knight was his nephew who had taken his dukedom and his lands and castle by force, and that none could stand against him. He, Liconal, was now too old to give him combat.

Yet there was to be an annual tournament the following day at which the prize would be a silver sparrow hawk. If it was won – and the Black Knight, whose name was Duke Ylder, had already won it twice – then it would be his to give to the fairest lady in all the land. Duke Ylder planned to give it to his lady.

Geraint said that if he could borrow armour he would fight Duke Ylder but Liconal told him that he could only enter if he had a lady to whom he could give the prize. At this Geraint said that there was none so fair as Enid and that if she would consent he would fight and give her the silver sparrow hawk, and she would always be his lady. If he lost, then she would have lost nothing. She smiled and agreed to attend.

At the tournament, after a mighty battle, Geraint won and gave the trophy to Enid. One would have thought that all would be well.

A champion spurned

After feasting with the vanquished duke and agreeing that Liconal and Ylder should go to King Arthur's court to settle their dispute, the party were about to set out. Enid imagined that Geraint would go with her and that they would be married and she would become his lady. Yet he told her that he could not go, for he was not yet a knight and must seek further adventures before he could return and become a knight. This angered Enid and she spurned him, calling him unworthy because he had deceived her into thinking that he was of a higher rank than he was.

He in turn was also angered and said that after her harsh words he could not possibly go back to Caerleon.

"If it pleases you, ride ahead of me, without looking back and without saying a word to me, no matter what occurs, and you will see what may chance."

Feeling that she had been harsh, Enid agreed. So they rode on and were confronted by a succession of robbing knights. On each occasion she was about to warn him, but he said:

"Say not a word, it may be that you wish these knights to kill me, but I shall fight them."

So he defeated and killed them; first three, then six and then nine knights. On each occasion he stripped the knights of their armour which he tied to their horses and ordered Enid to ride on ahead with them, never speaking a word to him.

Soon they were met by a knight, Sir Oringle of Limors, who invited them to stay in his castle. Sir Oringle said that Enid should part company with such a surly knight, for they never even exchanged a word between them. She said that in fact she would rather travel with no-one else.

Sir Oringle said that he could take her by force and kill Geraint if he desired, yet if she would come willingly, he would spare Geraint's life. Horrified by this she said that on the morrow they would ride out and she would hide from Geraint until Sir Oringle came.

The next morning they set off and once they had ridden out of the valley into a forest Enid turned and begged Geraint's pardon, for she knew that he had forbidden her to speak to him, but that to save him she had no option. She told him that they would be followed and that they should ride as fast as they could to escape. But Sir Oringle and his men were already on the road and could be heard approaching in the mist. Geraint refused to run and said that he would stand and fight.

This time Sir Oringle had four score knights accompanying him. He cried out that if Geraint yielded and the Lady Enid came to him of her own free will, then he could go free. Geraint charged and unhorsed Sir Oringle, and then charged into the eighty knights, fighting furiously and killing many. Yet there were too many and he was unhorsed and ended up unmoving on his back, with many wounds.

Sir Oringle recovered and ordered that the dead should be carried back to the castle, and he took Enid.

Not a morsel nor a sip

That night Sir Oringle held a feast. He sat at the table with Enid at his side. He ordered that the body of Geraint should be brought in and laid on a bower at one end of the hall.

"He fought, but he was overcome by the better knight. Now, Lady Enid, you can be my wife. Come, eat, and drink."

"I will not. Not a single morsel, nor a single sip will I ever have until first I see Geraint take."

"That is impossible, for he is dead!" cried Sir Oringle. And growing angrier at her obstinacy he threatened her, and then struck her. She screamed and the sound woke Geraint from his deep swoon. He leapt up, grabbed his sword and jumped onto the table and struck Sir Oringle's head clean off his shoulders. All Sir Oringle's men fled from the hall, for it seemed as if a dead man had come back to life.

Geraint and Enid returned to Caerleon and were met by Sir Kay, who was rude to Geraint and was put firmly in his place by him. Sir Gawain watched and said that Geraint had behaved appropriately, and that Sir Kay had been in the wrong.

Meanwhile King Arthur and his knights had caught the stag and Geraint was given its head, as promised, so that he could give it to his lady. He and Enid were wed and Geraint was knighted and took his seat at the Round Table.

Sir Gawain and Dame Ragnell

On Christmas Day one year the court had assembled at Carlisle, after King Arthur's army had fought a great battle against the Saxons.

A fair damsel came running in to the court and curtsied before the king.

"Oh good King Arthur, I beg that you send your worthiest knight to rescue my dear husband." And she told of how she and her husband had been riding the day before near Castle Hewin, which lies overlooking Tarn Wathelyne. A dark knight had challenged and defeated her husband and taken him prisoner. He had struck her several times across the face, which all present could see, for she had weals on both cheeks.

"I told him that I would seek justice from King Arthur's court, for I knew that you would be here in Carlisle. He laughed at me and told me that the cowardly King Arthur would never dare to come himself. And so I came as quickly as I could, Sire, to see if you could send a worthy knight."

King Arthur was incensed and stood up.

"It is long since I have taken a quest myself, but this one I shall. I shall teach that craven rogue a lesson with my sword and my spear."

A tale of courtly love

Here is another tale of courtly love, which comes from a Fifteenth Century poem. It is often compared with an earlier version included in the Fourteenth Century poet Geoffrey Chaucer's *The Wife of Bath's Tale*. It also has parallels with *Sir Gawain and the Green Knight*. It is certainly an apocryphal tale which fits well in the Arthurian canon.

And calling for his sword Excalibur and Ron, his spear, he made ready to set off straight away. Sir Lancelot and Sir Gawain begged to go in his place in case there was treachery afoot but he would not hear of it. He followed the lady through the dark Inglewood and across dark lands until they came to Tarn Wathelyne and the Castle Hewin.

The portcullis rose and a fearsome knight came out riding upon a huge war horse. King Arthur set his spear in place and charged. But he had not even reached the drawbridge when his own horse rose up on its hind legs, snorting with fear, its eyes open wide and rolling in terror.

King Arthur also for the first time in his life felt true terror and his limbs seemed to stop working.

"What...what evil is this?" he gasped. "This is devil's work."

The dark knight roared with laughter. "You are defeated by Sir Gromer Somer Joure, the Knight of Tarn Wathelyne. None may withstand the terror within me. I am the champion of Morgan le Fay and this is her castle."

"Have mercy and pity on me," King Arthur gasped.

"Aye, I will have pity on you, for I am a true knight and am obliged to serve whoever I may serve at the time. Give me your word that you will return here in one year, on your own. I give you a riddle that you have one year to find the answer to. Meet me here with the correct answer and I will spare your life. If you do not have that answer then you will lose your head here on this magic bridge, and I will toss your remains into the dark waters of this tarn."

"As a knight and a king, I give you my word."

"Then go, and answer this twelve months hence – what is it that all women most desire?"

The king returns to meet his fate

On his way back King Arthur met with Sir Gawain, who had ridden after him. He told him of his meeting with Sir Gromer Somer Joure.

"Good nephew, I do not know the answer and I do not know what to do to avoid my fate, for I am honour bound to return in twelve months."

"We must ask all the women that we can, my Lord," replied Sir Gawain. And over the next year they asked all the women that they met the same questions until they received enough answers to fill two books.

As Christmas approached the following year King Arthur and Sir Gawain journeyed towards Tarn Wathelyne. On the way they met a lady dressed in fine clothes riding towards them on a fine white horse. However, as she drew near they both cringed, for she was the most loathsome and repellent looking creature they had ever seen. She was toad-like with a fat abdomen, coarse features, large slobbering lips like a big fish, and wide staring, red-rimmed eyes.

Despite their revulsion they treated her courteously, as honourable knights should. The crone cackled.

"Welcome, King Arthur. I know who you are and what errand you are on. I can help you, for I know the answer to your riddle. I can tell you if you promise me one wish."

"What is your will, my lady?"

"That you will give me one Knight of the Round Table, nobly born, to be my husband this same day."

King Arthur was crestfallen. "That I cannot grant, my lady." But Sir Gawain immediately agreed to marry the lady, whose name was Dame Ragnell. And so she told King Arthur the secret answer and he rode off alone with his books filled with answers.

Sir Gromer Somer Jure was waiting for him. Arthur gave him all of the answers that he had accumulated in the book.

The dark knight drew his sword. "These are all wrong. Women truly do not want fine clothes, riches or any of these baubles or trinkets that they say they do. Bow your head, King Arthur and prepare to die."

"Wait! I have another answer," King Arthur said, preparing to give Dame Ragnell's secret reply. "I met a loathsome woman on the moor as I came here. She told me that what all women desire most is to rule over men."

Sir Gromer Somer Jure sheathed his sword and let out a dreadful oath. "We have been betrayed by that witch Dame Ragnell! Yet as a true knight I say that you have answered correctly and so I set you free." He wheeled his horse round and prepared to go back into the castle. "Perhaps one day when I am free I can serve you, for I am a true knight."

King Arthur watched him return to the castle and the portcullis fell. He then returned to Sir Gawain and Dame Ragnell.

"Ha! I have saved you this day," the crone cackled. "Now this knight must fulfil his part of the bargain."

A choice

After much rejoicing to see their king return the court was silent when it beheld the loathsome Dame Ragnell. Their immediate wedding was greeted with pity and none could look happily on Sir Gawain for all felt that he had been tricked by an ogre.

Yet Sir Gawain married Dame Ragnell and after the wedding feast took her to his chamber that night.

"Now kiss me, husband," she said when they were alone.

Sir Gawain steeled himself, closed his eyes and did so. Then he turned away as she cackled at his reaction. Then all went quiet and in place of her coarse voice he heard a sweet voice instead. "Sir Gawain, my lord and husband, you have released me." In amazement he turned to see a beautiful damsel before him.

"You have released me from the magic spell cast upon my brother and I by Morgan le Fay." And she told him of how Sir Gromer Somer Joure, her brother, was also bewitched to do Morgan le Fay's bidding.

He took her in his arms and kissed her fondly, falling deeply in love with her as he did so.

"Yet I am not entirely free," she whispered. "You have a choice to make. I can only be like myself twelve hours of each day. So you can choose to have me like this in the day when I may be seen at court and you will not be embarrassed by my ugliness, or you can have me like this when we are alone."

Sir Gawain bowed to her. "My lady, that choice is not mine, but yours. Whichever gives you the least discomfort will be the choice to make."

At this she threw herself into his arms and wept. "Oh good Sir Gawain, my lord, in giving up your choice you have undone the spell.

I am as I now am forever. And we may have many years of happiness before us."

And indeed they did, for seven years, when she disappeared from Camelot for ever. No one knew for certain what had happened, whether she had died or run away. But there are those who thought that she ran away from the eyes of men because she was pregnant, and that she felt that she needed to bring her child up by herself.

That child, some said, would grow up to be one of the very finest of Knights – Sir Percival of Wales, one of the three Grail Knights.

Chapter Three

The Quest for the Holy Grail

*The cup, the cup itself, from which our
Lord
Drank at the last sad supper with his
own.
This, from the blessed land of Aromat –
After the day of darkness, when the dead
Went wandering o'er Moriah – the good saint
Arimathaean, Joseph, journeying brought
to Glastonbury, where the winter thorn
Blossoms at Christmas, mindful of our
Lord.
And there awhile it bode; and if a man
Could touch or see it, he was heal'd at
once,
By faith, of all his ills. But then the times
Grew to such evil that the holy cup
Was caught away to Heaven, and dis-
appear'd.*
The Holy Grail, Idylls of the King,
Alfred, Lord Tennyson

ONCE again the fellowship of the Round Table had gathered at
Camelot to celebrate the Feast of Pentecost. In the evening they
were seated in the Great Hall when a lady rode in on a white
horse. She saluted King Arthur.

"Sire, in God's name, where is Sir Lancelot?" she asked.

"He is yonder," the king directed her.

She went to Lancelot and told him that King Pelles sent him his
regards, and then she requested that he should follow her into the
forest. He did so and eventually they came to an abbey. He was shown

into a chamber where Sir Bors and Sir Lionel had been resting on their way to Camelot.

Twelve nuns came in, leading the youth Galahad. They asked Sir Lancelot to make him a knight. Lancelot, knowing that Galahad was his son, agreed to do so. Thus, after keeping a vigil overnight before the altar, a requisite to being knighted, Galahad was knighted the next day by Sir Lancelot.

Galahad declined the offer to ride to Camelot with Sir Lancelot, Sir Bors and Sir Lionel, telling them that he would come soon.

When they arrived back at Camelot and the fellowship was about to take their seats again, golden writing appeared on the Siege Perilous:

Who knows what the Holy Grail looked like?

Four hundred and fifty-four years after the passion of our Lord Jesus Christ this siege should be filled.

Sir Lancelot suggested that it should be covered with a cloth until the worthy knight arrived to take it.

It was Pentecost and King Arthur was reminded that it was his custom to await some strange happening or some quest. Almost immediately, the company was alerted by a squire to a strange phenomenon; a block of stone was floating in the river and a sword with a golden handle shaped like a cross was embedded in it. They proceed to the river and saw written on the sword:

Never shall man take me hence but only he by whose side I ought to hang, and he shall be the best knight in the world.

King Arthur assumed that this knight must be Sir Lancelot, but Lancelot refused to try to remove it, because of his forbidden love for Queen Guinevere. Next King Arthur instructed first Sir Gawain and then Sir Percival, but neither could remove it.

When they returned to the Great Hall an old man came in with Sir Galahad. He instructed the nearest knight to remove the cloth from the Siege Perilous, and it was found that the gold letters had changed:

The reason why the Holy Grail must be found

The great quest for the holy vessel may seem obscure, except that religion was incredibly important in the days when the tales were being written. But there are three main points that have to be considered, which are interlinked and which may make it seem more in keeping with the modern idea of an adventure story.

- The Dolorous Stroke resulted in three lands being laid to waste
- These lands, The Waste Lands, can only be restored by the blood of Christ and the coming of the Holy Grail
- The Maimed King, often known as the Fisher King, can only be cured by the blood of Christ from the Spear of Longinus

---

This is the siege of Sir Galahad the High Prince.

Galahad removes the sword from the floating stone, Arthur Rackham, 1917.

So, Sir Galahad then took his seat and they had their feast. Afterwards, King Arthur took Galahad down to the river and showed him the marvellous sight of the sword in the stone block. Sir Galahad was not surprised and pointed out that he had no sword in his empty scabbard. He removed the sword easily and sheathed it, saying, "Now have I the sword that struck the Dolorous Stroke."

A joust was then held at which Sir Galahad, without a shield, defeated all comers except Lancelot, Gawain, Percival and Bors, whom he did not fight. Sir Galahad had arrived.

Then they were all shown a vision of the Holy Grail and once it had gone Sir Gawain vowed that he would go forth and search for it. The other

Knights of the Round Table made the same vow and, on the following day, 140 of them left Camelot upon the Quest for the Holy Grail.

Knights of the Round Table and the Holy Grail, Fifteenth Century.

Sir Galahad's Adventures

The fresh young knight Sir Galahad rode out, still without a shield, and soon ran into adventure.

At an abbey he met King Bagdemagus and Sir Uwaine. They told him that they had heard about a marvellous shield that was held in the abbey. It was said that no-one could carry it for more than three days without evil befalling them.

The next day they were shown the shield, which was as white as snow except for a red cross at its centre. King Bagdemagus insisted upon taking it to see how he fared. Not far from the abbey he was challenged to joust by a knight in white armour, and was unhorsed and wounded.

The Three Grail Knights

Although one hundred and forty Knights of the Round Table set out upon the Quest for the Holy Grail there were only three who were good enough to be involved in obtaining it. They each had a part to play. This would involve the healing of King Pelles, the Fisher King.

- Sir Galahad – who would attain the Grail
- Sir Percival – who must overcome envy and jealousy and cultivate humility
- Sir Bors – must overcome guilt at leaving his brother Sir Lionel to his fate

---

The knight instructed his squire to take the wounded king back to the abbey with the shield, for it belonged to none but Sir Galahad.

Sir Galahad rode out with the shield and met the white knight who told him of the shield's origin.

"It was made four hundred years ago in the city of Sarras in the Holy Land. It was brought to Britain by Joseph of Arimathea by an enchanted ship. When he lay dying he painted that cross with his own blood and ordered that it should be held behind the altar in this abbey until its rightful owner came to collect it. Go now, Sir Galahad, true knight of God, for your quest has begun."

After several other adventures he met a damsel who told him that he must board the Enchanted Ship to attain the Holy Grail. There he would be joined by Sir Percival and Sir Bors.

Sir Percival's Adventures

Sir Percival met a knight with a white shield with a red cross, and was unhorsed by him. He was bemused as to who it could be, for no-one had ever beaten him before, apart from Sir Lancelot. When he recovered he attempted to follow the mysterious knight. He was angry and jealous of Sir Galahad.

He met a hermit who told him that he was following Sir Galahad and that they both had a destiny, and that destiny was the Holy Grail. If he could help to find it then he would one day meet again with the Lady Blanchefleur.

He rode out and was set upon by twenty knights who had no love of the Round Table. He killed seven, but was unhorsed and his horse killed. Then from out of the forest came Sir Galahad who defeated the others before riding off, leaving Percival alone.

He had more adventures and was tempted by demons but through prayer and devotion they were swept away.

A nun appeared and told him that he had passed the tests and might board the Enchanted Ship.

Sir Bors' Adventures

Sir Bors de Gannis, cousin to Sir Lancelot, had ridden out of Camelot and met a recluse who told him that to obtain the Grail he must learn to be pure of heart. The recluse instructed him in many things, among them that to be pure he must forgo pleasures of the flesh and only eat bread and drink water. He told him that although he was not a great knight, yet purity and good living was more important than glory in jousts or on the battlefield.

When Sir Bors was ready he rode off again and saw two knights leading a horse upon which was a wounded and bleeding knight. They were flogging him with thorns. To his horror Sir Bors saw that it was his brother, Sir Lionel.

He was about to give battle when a damsel cried out for she was being carried off by a knight. Sir Bors was in a dilemma but decided to rescue the damsel first and then rescue his brother. He pursued the knight, they fought and Sir Bors delivered him a mortal blow. He then wanted to

How at the Castle of Corbin a Maiden Bare in the Sangreal and foretold the Achievements of Galahad, by Dante Gabriel Rossetti, 1864.

rescue his brother but the damsel beseeched him to escort her home for it was getting dark.

At her tower she and other maidens tempted him with food, drink and pleasures of the flesh but, good knight that he was, he resisted. The tempting maidens were demons and were swept away.

Sir Bors continued on his way the next morning and approached an abbey. An armoured knight approached him and he was delighted to see that it was his brother, Sir Lionel. Yet Sir Lionel was full of anger and spite for him, since he had ignored his plight. Sir Bors pled for forgiveness.

Sir Lionel was not in a forgiving mood and meant to have his brother's life, either hacking him down as a coward or in fair combat. Yet Sir Bors was full of guilt and would not fight. He submitted himself to whatever Sir Lionel would do. A monk came from the abbey and remonstrated with Sir Lionel, begging him not to behead Sir Bors. In blind rage Sir Lionel smote the monk's head from his shoulders.

In that instant there was a wind and the demon that had possessed Sir Lionel departed. A hermit appeared and explained that they were being tested. Sir Lionel was to stay at the abbey for a year to do penance for his crime but Sir Bors must continue his important quest.

He rode off and came to the sea-shore where he saw the Enchanted Ship. He boarded it, met Sir Percival, and then it immediately sailed away. The ship was full of wonders, fully lit and with fine linens and couches.

Bors and Percival told each other of their adventures and Sir Percival informed Sir Bors that now they only needed Sir Galahad. The Enchanted Ship sailed on to the place where the third Grail Knight would come aboard.

Sir Bors and Sir Lionel.

Sir Lancelot's Adventures

Sir Lancelot rode a long way in his quest to find Castle Carbonek again, for he had been there before and had seen the Holy Grail.

After much travelling, he came to a cross where two paths met. The light was fading and he was weary. He dismounted and noted that there was a slab of white marble at the base of the cross. Then Lancelot saw a small chapel not far away and went to see if he could find someone who could tell him where he was. The chapel was ancient, crumbling and covered in ivy. He walked round it and saw a light shining from a high window. He hammered on the door to see if he could attract the attention of whoever was inside, but there was no reply. Then he climbed up the ivy to look inside and was surprised to see an altar with a large branched silver candlestick containing six flickering candles. He was seized by a burning desire to go inside to look at the altar and perform his devotions before it, but could not climb through the window. He climbed down and tried the door again, to no avail. With a sigh of resignation, for he was sleepy and felt his strength failing, he returned to his horse by the cross. Then he took off his helmet, took care of his horse's needs, lay down with his shield for a pillow and went to sleep at the base of the cross.

Lancelot was not sure whether he was dreaming or whether he was in a half-doze. The door of the chapel opened and a hermit came out carrying the candlestick which he placed on the white marble slab. A sick knight rode up and dismounted. Clearly he was in great pain and instantly sank to his knees.

"Ah, sweet Lord!" he said to the cross. "When will this pain leave me? When will you allow the Holy Grail to come to take away my pain, which I have suffered with for so long?"

And then a salver appeared and upon it was the Holy Grail.

The knight made the sign of the cross and then on hands and knees crawled towards it and touched the holy vessel. Miraculously, he was cured and able to stand.

The hermit and other figures picked up the Holy Grail, the candlestick and the salver and returned them to the chapel. The knight knelt and prayed in front of the cross. By the time he had finished the hermit had reappeared.

"Thanks be to God that I am cured and am well again," the knight said. Then in wonder he pointed at Sir Lancelot. "Yet how is it that this knight, who looks as if he belongs to the fellowship of the Round Table, could lie there sleeping while the Holy Grail was within his reach?"

"Because he is weighed down with sins," the hermit replied. "He cannot move and could not enter the Chapel of the Holy Grail, nor could he move to reach it when it came to you here. He has been found wanting."

The Failure of Sir Lancelot to enter the Chapel of the Holy Grail, one of a number of Holy Grail tapestries woven by Morris & Co 1891-1894 for Stanmore Hall.

Sir Lancelot found himself weeping at the sound of this and wept in his sleep until he awoke in the early morning. Then the hermit spoke with him and Lancelot made a confession of his sins; of his love for Queen Guinevere and of his guilt over his relationship with Elaine.

The hermit told him that he had been found wanting, which was a great pity because he above all other knights had been granted strength, health, intelligence and a good heart by God, yet he had allowed himself to sin. It would be doubtful if he would be able to achieve the Quest of the Holy Grail, but yet he should try. It was more likely that the quest would be achieved by Sir Galahad, whom he would soon meet and whom he should acknowledge as his son by Elaine.

The hermit gave Lancelot a shirt of horse hair to wear, to help him avoid further temptations of the flesh, for it would hurt and chaff his skin and always remind him that he should do good for the love of God.

After several further adventures he met the knight with the white shield and red cross, and to his amazement was defeated by him in a friendly joust. Realising that it must be Sir Galahad he chased after him. Eventually he came to the sea-shore where the Enchanted Ship was waiting. On board he found Sir Galahad, Sir Percival, Sir Bors and Sir Percival's sister.

Sir Percival's sister

Sir Percival's sister was versed in the history of the Grail, Joseph of Arimathea and the Enchanted Ship. She told them something of what might happen to each of them, but of her own fate she was reticent and seemed sad. She told them that before they arrived at the Waste Lands, they must go to a castle wherein an ill lady resided in a tower.

The ship coasted into a bay and they went ashore, following Percival's sister through a forest to a castle. An armed knight awaited them. He asked them whether or not Percival's sister was a virgin.

"Sir, I am a maid, for I have vowed to be a nun in the service of the Lord my whole life."

At this the knight seized her and demanded that she fulfil an old custom demanded of all maids that visit the castle.

"Every maid who comes here must give enough of her blood to fill a special vessel that we have."

The four Round Table knights were horrified and prepared to fight, but a large body of armed knights come out of the castle and with them a damsel carrying a large vessel. Outnumbered and out-armed they fought, almost unto death, when another knight came from the castle and bid them stop fighting. He explained that if they were to go into the castle of their own free will there would be no more bloodshed.

They agreed, and it transpired that the lady of the castle was afflicted by a magical spell and was suffering from a leprosy-like condition. Only blood from a pure virgin could cure her.

Percival's sister agreed, for she was aware of her impending fate. She gave her blood but her wound could not be staunched and she slowly bled to death. Her last wish was to be buried in Sarras, which is where Galahad would be buried one day.

Sir Gawain's role in the quest

The worthy Sir Gawain was told by the hermit Naciens that he would not be found spiritually pure enough to attain the Holy Grail, but his worthiness was such that he would be able to release the Waste Lands from the evil magic that had suppressed them.

The lady of the castle was cured and Percival's sister was carried to the Enchanted Ship which would carry her to Sarras. When they returned to the castle they found that it had been burned by bolts from beyond, a punishment for the deaths of so many maids, for their tombs were found in the little nearby chapel.

The knights separated on further adventures. Before they departed they wished each other luck and good fortune and prayed to meet again at Carbonek.

The end of the Quest for the Holy Grail

The three Grail Knights, Percival, Bors and Galahad met again and stumbled across the Castle Carbonek. It was just as Percival remembered it. King Pelles was still lying on his couch with his knights about him. Naciens the hermit was by his side.

Naciens told them that within the enchanted castle of Carbonek the Holy Grail would be found, but first they must feast. The three knights refused the fine food and drink and took only bread and water.

Then the Grail procession appeared in the form of three maidens who walked in a trance-like state. They were carrying the Holy Grail, the salver and the spear of Longinus. Percival recognised Blanchefleur as one of the maidens.

Sir Galahad took out his sword and, holding it in front of him, joined the procession. Naciens then indicated that the two other knights should follow with King Pelles, and they picked up his couch and carried him between them out of the hall and into the chapel. There Naciens the hermit revealed himself as the Priest of the Grail, who had lived for centuries, in penance for having wronged Joseph of Arimathea. He handed the Grail to Sir Galahad, who drank from it. Then Naciens passed away peacefully.

Then with the spear of Longinus Sir Galahad dropped the blood of Christ into the grievous, unhealed wound of King Pelles – who was, of course, his grandfather – and the wound healed.

Then one of the Grail maidens brought a sword that had been broken into three pieces to Percival. Many knights had tried to repair it, but none had succeeded. Percival prayed first and then was able to repair it. Then Percival and Blanchefleur were united and married by Sir Galahad who was now the Priest of the Grail, after the passing of Naciens.

Having gained the Grail and healed King Pelles, Sir Galahad's soul passed from his body and he passed away. And as he did so, so the Holy Grail, the salver and the spear disappeared. Sir Bors carried the body of Sir Galahad to the Enchanted Ship and sailed with it to Sarras where he buried it next to that of Percival's sister.

He then returned to Camelot and told King Arthur all about his adventures and those of Sir Galahad and Sir Percival. King Arthur ordered that all of these chronicles should be written down as volumes on *The History of the Holy Grail* and placed in the library at Salisbury.

Alternate endings to the quest for the Holy Grail

This tale has several different endings, which is not surprising. The main alternative is that the three Grail Knights travelled on the Enchanted Ship to Sarras, taking the Grail with them from Britain back to the Holy Land. And there Galahad and Percival died and were buried by Sir Bors, who returned to Camelot and aided Lancelot at the end.

In Malory's *Le Morte d'Arthur*, Sir Percival and Sir Bors left and went to a hermitage where Percival took holy orders and devoted himself to God. Bors stayed with him but remained secular, for it was his intention to return one day to Camelot. A year and two days later, Percival died and Sir Bors buried him beside his sister and Sir Galahad before he returned to Camelot.

Chapter Four

The Death of Arthur

*Then spoke King Arthur, breathing
heavily:
"What is it thou hast seen? or what hast
heard?"*

The Passing of Arthur, Idylls of the King,
Alfred, Lord Tennyson

THIS tale has several versions and what follows gives an overview of them. Most emphasise the relationship between Queen Guinevere and Sir Lancelot and the effect that it had on the whole edifice of Camelot.

It is not a happy-ever-after fairy tale, but a brooding tale, filled with a sense that King Arthur's vision of a great country, wisely ruled and at peace is doomed to fade away as the fellowship of the Round Table crumbles.

Lancelot and Guinevere

After the quest for the Holy Grail there were many empty seats at the Round Table. King Arthur knew that they would never be filled again and that Merlin's prophesy was coming true.

Yet for a while there seemed to be peace and the people were happy. But two people were anything but happy, for Lancelot and Guinevere had entered that part of their relationship when they yearned for each other but knew that they could never honourably express that love.

At court everyone was aware that they had strong feelings for each other, except King Arthur. He could not believe that the two people who meant so much to him could even contemplate betrayal.

The fairy tale image of Lancelot and Guinevere.

Sir Lancelot tried to distance himself from the Queen and performed many quests on behalf of other women. This angered Queen Guinevere and she called him to her.

"Sir Lancelot, I have noticed that you ride to help damsels and other gentlewomen. Is your love for me growing cold?"

He replied that he was sorry to have given that impression. "Yet it must be so," he went on. "When I was on the Quest for the Holy Grail I realised how sinful my love for you was."

This angered the Queen even more and she ordered him to leave her. And so, with much sorrow Sir Lancelot rode out of Camelot. Queen Guinevere tried to keep up a brave face and spent time with her ladies by riding out herself and collecting May blossom.

There was a knight called Sir Melliagraunce, the son of a king, who had lusted after Queen Guinevere for a long time but had done nothing because he feared Sir Lancelot. But now that Sir Lancelot had gone, seemingly for good, he took his opportunity and rode out with twenty knights and ambushed the Queen and her party of ladies and knights.

Her knights fought for her but were soon wounded, for they were without armour. Sir Melliagraunce threatened to have them killed unless she submitted to him.

On the promise that they would be spared, she rode with him and his men to his castle where her knights were imprisoned. She managed, however, to give a squire her ring and he escaped, despite having arrows fired and spears thrown at him.

Meanwhile a wounded knight by the name of Sir Urry had been brought to Camelot with three fearsome head wounds. It was said that only the noblest knight in the land could heal him. King Arthur sent out squires to bring Sir Lancelot home. Despite protesting that he was not the noblest knight, Sir Lancelot obeyed King

Queen Guinevere collecting May blossom, by John Collier, 1900.

Arthur's command and attempted to lay his hands on the wounded knight to heal him. Soon the wounds began to heal.

The squire then arrived with Queen Guinevere's ring and upon hearing the tale Sir Lancelot leapt on his horse and galloped to save her. On the road he was attacked by robbers with bows, who shot his charger from under him. They fled before he could reach them, which was as well for them.

Now on foot and heavily armed he made his way to the castle of Sir Melliagraunce. Soon a cart with two woodsmen came along the road. When he asked to be taken in their cart one insolently told him that Sir Melliagraunce would never allow it, and he lashed out with his whip. It was a foolish move against an armoured knight, for Sir Lancelot smote him dead with one swipe of his gauntlet. The other woodsman begged for his life and obeyed Sir Lancelot's order to turn the cart around and take him to the castle.

One of Queen Guinevere's ladies saw the cart approaching with a knight in it and she exclaimed:

"Good madam, there is a cart coming for the hangman. But strangely, there is a knight in the cart."

This was such an unusual thing, for no knight ever travelled in a cart, unless he was being dragged to his execution for some heinous crime, but when Queen Guinevere saw who it was she was greatly relieved. "I knew that he would come to save me!" she sighed with relief.

Sir Lancelot hammered on the castle door. "Come out, false knight and meet your doom."

Sir Melliagraunce, seeing who it was, ran to Queen Guinevere and begged her forgiveness and asked that she would intercede for him. This she agreed to do and when Sir Lancelot was admitted she calmed him down, despite his desire to kill the treacherous knight. King Arthur and his knights arrived and the King heard all that had happened and agreed that the two knights should do battle a week later at Camelot.

Along with the king and the other knights, Sir Lancelot accepted the knight's hospitality. He agreed to be shown around the castle by Sir Melliagraunce himself. Along a corridor they went until Sir Lancelot stepped upon a concealed trap door that sent him hurtling onto a pile of straw in a deep dungeon.

King Arthur and Queen Guinevere returned to Camelot with their entourage of knights. No-one thought that Sir Lancelot's disappearance was odd, for he often went off on his own without warning. They did not know that he had been kept prisoner in Sir Melliagraunce's dungeon, given food and water by a damsel.

When the day of the combat arrived, Sir Melliagraunce presented himself with some show of false valour. He knew full well that if Sir Lancelot did not appear, he would be regarded as the victor and Sir Lancelot would be dishonoured as a coward. What he had not bargained on was the damsel falling in love with Sir Lancelot and agreeing to release him for the price of a kiss.

The appointed hour was almost past when Sir Lancelot rode up and informed the king of Sir Melliagraunce's infamy. At that the knight charged and they did battle, until Sir Lancelot unhorsed him, and then on foot delivered a mighty stroke that cleaved the false knight's skull in two. Thus did Sir Melliagraunce meet his end.

King Arthur was relieved to have his best knight back. As for Queen Guinevere, it inflamed her passion for Sir Lancelot and she contrived for him to meet her that evening. So began their affair.

Mordred and Agravaine

Sir Lancelot was not loved by all knights. There were some such as Sir Mordred and Sir Agravaine who were jealous of him. Agravaine heard of the love trysts between Sir Lancelot and Queen Guinevere, and together with Sir Mordred he contrived to raise ill feelings against the lovers. Agravaine asked his brother Sir Gawain to help them unmask their deceit before the King. Sir Gawain refused, for he loved both the queen and Sir Lancelot.

They petitioned King Arthur himself, who was distraught to hear of his wife's adultery and agreed that it was only correct that they should be treated the same way as any other of his subjects that were guilty of wrong doing.

"Take twelve knights and do what must be done," he said.

Sir Bors, Sir Lancelot's cousin, had a bad feeling that some ill was about to happen. He counselled his cousin not to visit the queen, but Sir Lancelot answered that he was not going to be long.

Mordred, Agravaine and the twelve knights waited until Sir Lancelot had gone into the queen's chamber, then hammered on the door.

"Come out, traitorous knight, you are undone!" cried Sir Mordred.

Sir Lancelot was unarmed and would stand little chance against fourteen armed and armoured knights. He talked with them and they assured him that if he came out they would take him prisoner and take him before the king.

Then Sir Lancelot wound his cloak around his arm and with his sword in his hand opened the door wide enough to permit one knight to enter. Sir Colgrevaunce rushed at him and struck at him. Sir Lancelot parried the blow and struck a single mortal blow to the knight. In a moment he dragged him through the door and bolted it again.

Queen Guinevere helped to remove Sir Colgrevaunce's armour and helped Sir Lancelot on with it. Then he threw open the door and charged into the knights with his sword flashing hither and thither. Sir Agravaine was killed first and then the others, leaving only Sir Mordred to run away nursing a wound.

Sir Lancelot bade the queen farewell.

"I must go quickly, my lady," he said. "But if ever you have need of me, or if you are in danger, then I will return and rescue you."

Sir Mordred informed the king and Sir Gawain of all that had happened and of how Sir Lancelot had defied arrest and killed so many of the knights. He demanded that the queen should suffer the punishment that was required.

A trial was held and the strength of feeling against the queen was obvious.

"There can be only one just punishment," King Arthur agreed, although it pained him to say it. "She must be burned at the stake."

Sir Gawain could not believe what had happened and tried to see alternative explanations.

"Sir Lancelot killed your brother, Gawain," the king said to his nephew. "If he returns to try and save her he must suffer a dishonourable death."

"My Lord, I pray that I never see such a thing."

And he refused the King's request to lead the queen to the stake on the following day.

"Then you must see that your brothers do so in your stead," King Arthur said.

Sir Lancelot to the rescue

It was a sad day in Camelot. The stake was prepared and Queen Guinevere, dressed in a smock, was led out by Sir Gareth and Sir Gaheris, Sir Gawain's two brothers. The pyre was lit and the queen was made ready to be tied to the stake.

Sir Lancelot charged into the field, hacking at any who barred his way. Sir Gaheris and Sir Gareth, both of whom were unarmed and present reluctantly, were unfortunate enough to get in Sir Lancelot's way. He cut them down and killed them without even knowing who they were. Then plucking Queen Guinevere from her captors he rode off with her.

He and his followers, including Sir Lionel and Sir Bors, rode with him to his Castle of Joyous Garde in Wales.

Sir Gawain's vengeance and the Day of Destiny

Upon finding that his two bothers had been killed so brutally when they had been unarmed, Sir Gawain's love of Sir Lancelot turned to the deepest hatred. He vowed that he would personally kill Sir Lancelot or give his life up in trying.

King Arthur saw that his beloved realm, his fellowship of the Round Table and Camelot itself were all disappearing, much as Merlin had told him they would before he had been incarcerated by the sorceress Viviene. No longer as decisive and now much more easily swayed, he was easily persuaded by Sir Gawain, his nephew and Sir Mordred, ostensibly his nephew but in reality his son, that he should declare war on Sir Lancelot.

King Arthur raised his army and laid siege to Joyous Garde but after fifteen weeks there was no sign of the castle weakening. Eventually, however, after much taunting Sir Lancelot and his followers sallied forth and a battle ensued. During it Sir Gawain killed Sir Lionel and Sir Bors knocked King Arthur down and cried to Sir Lancelot: "Shall I end this all here, with one stroke of this sword?"

Sir Lancelot angrily replied:

"Put down that sword and touch not a hair on our noble King's head or I will slay you myself." And he helped his King back on his horse. As he did so he offered to surrender Guinevere provided that she would be treated courteously and forgiven, for the fault was all his. He in return would leave the country never to return.

And so a truce was settled and Sir Lancelot escorted the queen from the castle into her husband's keeping, and he and his knights left the country for Armorica in France.

The peace did not last because Sir Gawain could not bear to think that Sir Lancelot still lived. He petitioned the King, as did his many knights, and once again war was declared. King Arthur led his army to the Castle of Benwick in Armorica, leaving Camelot and Britain under the charge of Sir Mordred.

Three times Sir Lancelot and Sir Gawain fought and on each occasion Sir Lancelot won, wounding Sir Gawain badly. This, despite Sir Gawain having been given extra strength from dawn until noon, thanks to a special blessing that a holy man had bestowed upon him.

In the meantime, Sir Mordred let it be known that King Arthur had been slain while fighting overseas and that he should be the rightful king. He persuaded the Archbishop of Canterbury to crown him.

As king he felt that he needed a queen, and since he had lusted after Queen Guinevere for some years, despite the fact that she was his step-mother, he tried to force her to marry him. She persuaded him that she should go to London and prepare herself, but once she reached London she retreated to the Tower of London and her followers secured it. A messenger was sent to France. The Archbishop of Canterbury opposed Mordred and was forced to flee to Glastonbury.

Upon receiving the message King Arthur and his army gave up their siege and sailed for Dover, where Mordred was waiting for them. A great battle took place, during which Sir Gawain was mortally wounded.

As Sir Gawain lay dying all his hatred for Sir Lancelot disappeared and he called for writing implements to write him a last letter, asking for his forgiveness and praying that he would come home to assist the king, for had he been with them none of this would have happened.

"Come at once, for Mordred will soon gather other rebels about him. Of me all you will find is a grave. My noble Lancelot, I salute you."

He died in King Arthur's arms. Arthur wept all night. Then Sir Gawain was entombed in the crypt at Dover Castle.

The Day of Destiny and the final battle

Some days later King Arthur and his army camped upon the plain of Camlann while Mordred and his army gathered less than a mile away. To Arthur's mind this was a significant place, for it was not far from there that he had been taken by Merlin years before to obtain Excalibur.

He slept poorly, since he was aware of Merlin's prophesy, that many of his knights would fall, and that the land of Logres would pass into dark times. Already foreign Saxon invaders were again regrouping, awaiting the passing of Camelot.

In a dream he saw himself on a throne attached to a wheel, which revolved and threatened to topple him into darkness with a pit of serpents and vipers. From this he thought he awoke to find Sir Gawain and a group of ladies on whose behalf the knight had fought during his life. He tried to warn King Arthur not to fight, for if he did so both he and Sir Mordred would die. His best course was to make peace.

Arthur awoke properly and called his loyal knights Sir Lucan and Sir Bedivere to him. He explained what he had seen and told them to take two priests and go to Sir Mordred and make a month's period of truce between them. He even told them to offer to give him lands in order to avoid war. This they did, offering Cornwall and the area of Kent. More than that, after the death of King Arthur, he would become the king.

To seal the peace it was agreed that King Arthur and Sir Mordred would meet between the two armies, each attended by fourteen knights.

"If there is any sign of treachery, any sign of a weapon being drawn, then you must charge the traitors," Arthur ordered.

Similarly, Sir Mordred gave an order to charge should anyone draw a weapon.

They met as agreed, signed the truce and wine was brought so that they could drink together. But at that moment, as ill luck would have it, an adder appeared and bit one of Sir Mordred's knights. With a curse of pain he unthinkingly drew his sword and slew the snake.

The metal flashed in the light and Arthur's troops saw it and believed that treachery was afoot. They charged. Sir Mordred's army immediately reacted and charged and soon a battle was being waged on the Plain of Camlann.

All day it raged, many knights achieving honour and many being slain. Both Arthur and Mordred fought bravely. Eventually, there were only dead knights all around.

In the fading evening light King Arthur wept at the scene and he peered about him to try to see Sir Mordred, the cause of all this carnage. He saw him leaning on his sword amid a heap of dead bodies.

He cried to Sir Lucan: "Now give me my spear, for I see the traitor who has caused all this."

Sir Lucan tried to dissuade him. "Leave him, Sire, for there are three of us and only one of him. You have won the field. Remember your dream and Sir Gawain's warning.'

Mordred resting on his sword, H.J. Ford, 1907.

But King Arthur was determined to deal out justice to his traitorous son and called out to Sir Mordred, and he in turn saw the king and charged at him.

With his spear, which was called Ron, Arthur ran at his enemy. He attacked under Mordred's shield and ran him through, dealing him a mortal wound.

Realising he would die Mordred grasped the shaft of the spear and dragged himself along it until he was close enough to swing his sword. He dealt Arthur a dreadful blow upon the head so that it split his helmet and produced a grievous wound.

They both fell. Mordred died screaming and writhing in agony as King Arthur slipped silently to the ground. Sir Lucan and his brother Sir Bedivere ran to their king and carried him from the battlefield to a small chapel. Both were wounded and losing blood. Sir Lucan was the most grievously wounded, for he had an injury in his abdomen and his innards were gaping from it. He collapsed and died.

Mists were swiftly gathering from the sea and it was eerily red from all the blood that had been spilt.

How Mordred was Slain by Arthur, Arthur Rackham, 1917.

"Alas!" cried the king as he momentarily regained consciousness. "What an awful sight to see such a noble knight die of such a horrible wound, from trying to help me – especially when his need was greater than mine."

Sir Bedivere knelt by his brother knight and wept. At last King Arthur coaxed Sir Bedivere. "Cease your weeping, gentle knight, for your brother is past all travail. My time is short now and I have one last service that I must demand of you. Take my sword Excalibur and go over that ridge. You will find a dark lake there. Throw my sword into the waters and then come back and tell me what you see."

The moon was now out and Sir Bedivere took the sword to the water's edge and looked out over the moonlit water, rippling eerily in the breeze. Yet as he hefted the sword in his hand he saw all of the precious jewels gleaming in the handle and he found himself thinking:

"What good would throwing such a priceless sword do?" And he hid the sword in the rushes and hurried back to the King.

"Tell me now, what did you see?" Arthur asked.

"I saw nothing but the wind rippling the dark waters," Sir Bedivere replied.

"Then you do not speak the truth," King Arthur replied. "Now go again and throw the sword in the lake."

Sir Bedivere went again and once more he thought that it would do no good to throw the sword away. He returned to the King, who again demanded:

"Tell me what you saw."

"I saw only the wind causing the water to ripple," Bedivere lied.

"Ah! You traitor and liar!" King Arthur cried. "You have betrayed me twice. You, whom I loved and honoured. You were a Knight of the Round Table and yet now you would bring dishonour upon yourself and the Round Table all for the value of this sword. Now go again and throw the sword away, for I am dying and feeling the bitter cold of the air."

A third time Sir Bedivere went to throw the sword in the lake and this time he overcame the covetous thoughts in his mind to keep it. Feeling deeply

Sir Bedivere casts Excalibur into the Lake.

ashamed of himself he stood by the waters edge and threw Excalibur as far as he could.

The sword spun and gleamed in the moonlight and a hand and arm broke the surface of the water and caught the sword as it fell. Three times it brandished the sword in the air and then it sank beneath the water, the blade of the sword slowly descending until only the tip remained, and then that too vanished.

Sir Bedivere returned to King Arthur and told him what had happened and the King nodded. "It is as it should be. Yet I have tarried too long. Carry me to the water's edge."

Sir Bedivere gently raised the king on his back and carried him to the water's edge. Slowly a barge with many ladies upon it appeared out of the mist. Three of them were dressed in gowns with black hoods. They were all weeping.

"Now place me in the barge," Arthur said to Sir Bedivere.

The three ladies received the king and he was laid down, his head resting in the lap of one of the Ladies of the Isle of Avalon.

One of the ladies was Queen Morgan le Fay, another was the Queen of North Gaul and the third was the Queen of the Waste Lands. "Alas, brother, why have you been so long in coming to me," Morgan le Fay asked softly, her voice quaking with emotion. "The wound in your head has caught too much cold."

Sir Bedivere stood on the shore and watched as slowly the barge started to move off. "My Lord, what will become of me now that you are going?" he asked.

"Comfort yourself," replied the King. "Do as well as you must, for you remain to tell others that I still live. Yet I must go to the Vale of Avalon to have this grievous wound healed. If you never hear from me again, pray for my soul."

Sir Bedivere wept on his own for some time, then went off into the forest and spent the night wandering. In the morning he came back to the chapel and found a hermit praying over a new grave.

"Sir," he asked, "who have you buried in this grave?"

And the hermit – who was actually the Archbishop of Canterbury, who had been forced to flee to Glastonbury from Sir Mordred when he had threatened to chop off his head – told Bedivere that in the night a number of ladies had brought a dead body and lit a thousand candles

---

I will come again

Malory goes on to say that in some parts of England, the legend states that King Arthur told Sir Bedivere to tell the people that he was going to have his grievous wound healed on the Isle of Avalon, and that he would remain there, asleep, with some of his faithful knights. They would come again if ever Britain was in need of him.

The Ladies of Avalon included these three queens – Queen Morgan le Fay, the Queen of North Gaul and the Queen of the Waste Lands – but also Viviene, who had cast her spell on Merlin.

This is a legend that several writers have used, including C S Lewis in his book *That Hideous Strength*.

and given him a hundred blessings. And he had buried the body for them.

"Sir, that body was my lord, King Arthur."

And Sir Bedivere decided there and then to serve the rest of his days at the chapel, which was near Glastonbury, praying for his king and serving God.

Queen Guinevere, when she heard that King Arthur was dead, went with five ladies to Amesbury Abbey, where she became a nun. There she spent the rest of her days praying and fasting and doing great penance for all the wrongs that she had done.

The Dolorous Death

Sir Lancelot returned to England upon receiving Sir Gawain's letter and was devastated to hear, when he landed at Dover with a huge army, that Sir Gawain had died and that King Arthur and Sir Mordred were also both dead, after having fought a great battle in which one hundred thousand men had died.

Before going to Queen Guinevere he was counselled by Sir Bors to go and pay his respects to Sir Gawain's tomb at Dover Castle. He did this and stayed for many days dispensing favours to the people of Dover. At last he set off on his own across the country to find Queen Guinevere. By chance he came across Amesbury Abbey where she had become the Abbess and, at sight of him, she fainted.

When she recovered she told him that because of their love all the evil things had happened. She had renounced the world and must never set eyes on him again. He should return to France, marry and forget her.

Sir Lancelot could not countenance such a thing. He told her that he would follow her example and become a monk.

On his way back towards Dover, he came across a chapel between rocks where two hermits, one the Archbishop of Canterbury and the other, Sir Bedivere, were praying. He joined them along with seven other knights who found their way there.

Lancelot became a priest. Some years later he had a vision telling him he must go to Amesbury, where he would find that Guinevere had died and that it was his task to take her body to Glastonbury to bury it with her husband, King Arthur.

Arthur's tomb, the Last Meeting of Lancelot and Guinevere, by Dante Gabriel Rossetti, Nineteenth Century.

With his fellow priests he did this and then returned to the hermitage where he basically starved to death, taking only water. He died and his body was taken to Joyous Garde and interred in the chapel.

Constantine became King of Britain and tried to rally the remaining knights, but none had any heart for knighthood and dispersed to their own countries.

Sir Bors and Sir Hector travelled to the Holy Land and spent their days fighting. They both died on Good Friday.

Chapter Five

Who, What, Where and When in Arthur's Realm

A storm was coming, but the winds
were still,
and in the wild woods of Broceliande,
Before an oak, so hollow, huge and old
It look'd a tower of ruin'd masonwork,
At Merlin's feet the wily Vivien lay.

Merlin and Vivien, Idylls of the King,
Alfred, Lord Tennyson

Who are the characters in Arthur's realm?

THERE are a large number of them. Not surprisingly, since there are many different sources for the tales, there are many characters whose names have a variety of spellings. Alternate spellings will be given in the biographical notes that follow.

The personalities of some characters may change from source to source. Indeed, some characters change within the same source, as for example in Malory's *Le Morte d'Arthur*. Sometimes this may reflect character development, but also the individual's character may have been modified because of the needs of the individual tale. It must be remembered that Malory seemed to have taken tales from many earlier sources and amalgamated them into a continuous narrative. Sometimes he did not even attempt to alter characters' personalities.

Sir Kay is one such example, for he is at times a just and courteous knight and at other times a gruff, rude, bigoted individual. Viviene is another character who is duplicitous in the early story, for she tricks the wizard Merlin and causes him to vanish from the story forever, yet at the end she appears as one of the Ladies of Avalon who takes King

Arthur away. And, of course, Queen Guinevere is a highly complex character who is at one time loved, and at another time reviled by the whole of society except those who are faithful to Sir Lancelot. Yet at the end she renounces the world and devotes herself to God and pays penance for her illicit relationship with her champion knight.

The question as to whether we can pin Arthur himself down to a historical person is another matter that we shall discuss in Part Two (see page 191).

Accolon

Sir Accolon of Gaul is Morgan le Fay's lover. He is given Excalibur and its scabbard by her and is induced to fight a knight on behalf of Sir Outlake. This knight is actually King Arthur. Arthur manages to cut loose the scabbard, thereby causing Accolon to lose his invulnerability. Viviene makes Accolon drop Excalibur, which Arthur retrieves and then deals Accolon a mortal blow.

Agravaine

Sir Agravaine is one of the sons of King Lot of Orkney and Queen Morgawse. His brothers are Gawain, Gaheris and Gareth. King Arthur is his uncle and Sir Mordred is his half-brother. He marries Lady Laurel.

He is killed by Sir Lancelot as he escapes, after he, Mordred and a party of twelve knights fail to arrest Lancelot and Guinevere after they had been caught together.

Sir Agravaine
Alternative spelling: Agravain.

Angwish

King Angwish of Ireland.

Arthur

King Arthur Pendragon, son of Uther Pendragon and Igrayne. He is shown to be the true king of Britain after he draws a sword from a stone. He sleeps with his half-sister Morgawse (not knowing that she is his half-sister) and begets Mordred. He marries Guinevere and establishes the fellowship of the Round Table. He holds court at Camelot and Caerleon.

In his early reign he is helped by Merlin, who leads him to a lake where he is given the sword Excalibur by the Lady of the Lake. He is saddened when later on Merlin is ensnared by magic and sent into an eternal sleep by the sorceress, Viviene.

Arthur leads the Britons at several great battles, most notably at Mount Badon where he defeats a Saxon army.

His favourite knight, Sir Lancelot, commits adultery with Guinevere and thereby sets in motion a chain of events that will lead to the breakdown of the fellowship of the Round Table, to treason and treachery and ultimately to the final battle of Camlann where Arthur kills his son Sir Mordred and receives a mortal blow from him. He is taken to the Isle of Avalon to have his grievous wound treated and healed.

Bagdemagus

King Bagdemagus is a Round Table knight who is cousin to King Arthur. He is injured by the White Knight when he attempts to prove his worth by carrying the shield that was placed above an altar by Joseph of Arimathea. It is eventually used by Sir Galahad.

Balin and Balan

Sir Balin and Sir Balan are two brave knights who sadly bring about each other's death.

Sir Balin strikes the Dolorous Stroke that maims King Pelles and causes the devastation resulting in the Waste Lands.

Bedivere

Sir Bedivere is the last knight remaining after the great battle between the armies of Arthur and Mordred. As King Arthur lies dying he instructs Bedivere to cast Excalibur into the lake but on two occasions he hides the sword. On the third he casts it and witnesses it being caught by the hand in the lake.

The barge comes carrying the Ladies of Avalon and he helps place Arthur on the barge and watches it disappear, taking Arthur to be healed of his grievous wound.

In Malory's *Le Morte d'Arthur*, he wanders that night in the forest and then comes to a hermitage in the morning where he is told that a man's body was buried that night, after being brought by many ladies.

Bedivere, by Aubrey Beardsley, 1884.

Sir Bedivere

Alternative spellings: Bedevere, Bedwyr.

Bertilak

Bertilak de Hautdesert, the Knight of the Lake, is the knight who befriends Sir Gawain in *Sir Gawain and the Green Knight*.

Bors

Sir Bors de Gannis is brother to Sir Lionel and cousin to Sir Lancelot. He is a faithful and loyal friend to Lancelot throughout his life and through all of the tragedies that befall them. He is one of the Grail Knights who achieve sight of the Holy Grail.

Carados

Sir Carados of the Dolorous Tower is an evil and craven knight who is killed by Sir Lancelot. His brother, Sir Tarquyn, vows to have revenge on Sir Lancelot and so sets about capturing and imprisoning knights in the belief that eventually Lancelot will come to him.

Colgrevaunce

Sir Colgrevaunce is one of the knights charged by King Arthur to catch Sir Lancelot and Guinevere in the act of adultery. He charges into the room to take the unarmed Lancelot but is killed instantly. Sir Lancelot puts on Sir Colgrevaunce's armour and goes to defeat the rest of the arresting party, except for Sir Mordred who is wounded and escapes.

Cote Mal Tayle

Sir Brewnor le Noyr is given this derogatory name by the mischievous Sir Kay. The name is from his ill-fitting coat, which had belonged to his father and whom he has vowed to avenge. Malory tells his tale in *Le Morte d'Arthur*.

Danas

Sir Danas is a cowardly knight who has usurped the estates of his brother, Sir Outlake. He is challenged to fight by Sir Outlake, but Morgan le Fay arranges for King Arthur to fight for him against an unnamed knight who will actually be Sir Accolon.

Ector

Sir Ector is King Arthur's foster father and the father of Sir Kay.

> **Sir Ector**
> Alternative spelling: Hector.

Ector de Marris

Sir Ector de Marris is Sir Lancelot's half-brother. He succeeds King Ban as King of Benwick.

Sir Ector de Marris

Alternative spelling: Sir Hector de Marris.

Elaine

Queen Elaine is one of the daughters of Gorlois and Igrayne. She becomes the wife of Ban, King of Benwick, and mother of Lancelot.

Queen Elaine

Alternative spelling: Elayne.

Elaine

Lady Elaine is the daughter of King Pelles of Carbonek. She falls in love with Sir Lancelot, who carries her favours and fights for her but he gently spurns her love, for he loves only Queen Guinevere.

She enlists the services of a sorceress and appears as Guinevere, then sends a message to Sir Lancelot who goes to her and sleeps with her. She conceives and gives birth to Galahad.

Elaine is the Lady of Astolat who is carried downriver to Camelot, one of the subjects of the paintings by the Pre-Raphaelites.

Lady Elaine

Alternative spelling: Elayne.

Elizabeth

Queen Elizabeth is the sister of King Mark, wife of King Meliodas and mother of Tristram.

Enid

Lady Enid teats Geraint badly and falls in love with him as he defeats a series of enemies who are backed up by ever-increasing groups of knights. It is a great love story.

According to Chrétien de Troyes, she and Erec are the lovers.

Lady Enid

Alternative spelling: Enide.

The Fisher King

This character appears in many myths and legends. He is a king, identified in the main story as King Pelles, wounded by the Dolorous Stroke, either from the spear of Longinus or from the Dolorous Sword. The wound cannot be healed by ordinary methods, indeed it will only be healed by the Grail or the Grail Knight. The Waste Lands that are created by this act are ruled by the Fisher King.

Gaheris

Sir Gaheris is one of the five sons of King Lot of Orkney and Queen Morgawse. His brothers are Gawain, Agravaine and Gareth. King Arthur is his uncle and Sir Mordred is his half-brother.

He eventually marries Lady Lyones who has been saved by his brother, Sir Gareth. Sir Lancelot accidentally kills him when he rescues Queen Guinevere from the stake.

Galahad

Sir Galahad is the son of Sir Lancelot. He is the perfect knight who will achieve the

Sir Galahad, by Howard Pyle, 1910.

Holy Grail. He heals King Pelles with the blood of Christ and becomes a Priest of Heaven. He passes away as he leaves his mortal coil and rises to heaven.

Gareth

Sir Gareth is one of the five sons of King Lot of Orkney and Queen Morgawse. His brothers are Gawain, Agravaine and Gaheris. King Arthur is his uncle and Sir Mordred is his half-brother. He is involved in the tale of Gareth and Lynette. Sir Kay mischievously nicknamed him Beaumains, or the Knight of the Kitchen.

Sir Gareth is Sir Gawain's favourite brother. He is killed by Sir Lancelot when he rescues Queen Guinevere from the stake. It is his death that Sir Gawain most deplores.

Garlon

Sir Garlon is the invisible knight, killed by Balin.

Gawain

Sir Gawain is one of the greatest Knights of the Round Table. He is one of the sons of King Lot of Orkney and Queen Morgawse. His brothers are Agravaine, Gaheris and Gareth. King Arthur is his uncle and Sir Mordred is his half-brother.

Before Sir Lancelot, he was the ideal knight. He marries the Dame Ragnell and is involved in the great story *Sir Gawain and the Green Knight*. He loves Sir Lancelot like a brother, but when Lancelot accidentally kills his brothers Gareth and Gaheris he vows revenge. Before he dies on the beach at Dover he writes a letter to Sir Lancelot, begging his forgiveness and praying that he will come to aid King Arthur.

Sir Gawain

Alternative spelling: Gawaine.

Geraint

Sir Geraint is involved in one of the great romances of the Arthurian saga. He fights increasing numbers of knights, all the time ordering Lynette, who is riding in front of him, not to talk to him. They are clearly in love and when Sir Oringle tries to foist himself on Lynette, she devises a plan to get away. Geraint will not take the easy way out by trying to run for it, but faces Oringle and his eighty knights. He is overcome and falls into a death-like swoon, from which he is later awoken by Lynette's scream. He leaps up and beheads Oringle.

Sir Gawain of Orkney, Howard Pyle, 1903.

Gorlois, Duke of Cornwall

Gorlois is the husband of Igrayne. He is killed by Uther Pendragon, who sought Merlin's help to seduce Igrayne by disguising himself magically as Gorlois.

Gorlois and Igrayne have three daughters, Morgawse, Elaine and Morgan le Fay.

Gonemans

Sir Gonemans is the elderly knight who instructs Percival on knighthood and combat.

Gromer Somer Joure

Sir Gromer Somer Joure is the Knight of Tarn Wathelyne. He appears in the tale of Sir Gawain and Dame Ragnell. Both he and his sister Ragnell had been bewitched by Morgan le Fay.

Guinevere

Queen Guinevere is the daughter of King Leodegraunce, the ruler of Caemelarde. She marries King Arthur, who loves her deeply. She is well loved at court until her love for Sir Lancelot starts to upset the court. It spells doom for Camelot and the fellowship of the Round Table.

Malory tells *The Tale of the Poisoned Apples* in which Guinevere is framed for having poisoned some apples that nearly kill Sir Gawain. As a result she gains his enmity and that of many other knights.

> **Queen Guinevere**
>
> Alternative spellings: Guenevere, Guenever, Gwenhwyfar.

Igrayne

Igrayne is the wife of Gorlois, the Duke of Cornwall. She is seduced by Uther Pendgaron who later marries her. While married to Gorlois she gives birth to Morgawse, Elaine and Morgan le Fay. She also gives birth to Arthur, by Uther Pendragon.

> **Igrayne**
>
> Alternative spellings: Igraine, Ygraine.

Ironside

Sir Ironside is the Knight of the Red Lands in the tale of Gareth and Lynette.

Isolde

There are two Isoldes: Isolde of Ireland, King Mark's wife, who falls in love with Sir Tristram and drinks a love potion with him; and Isolde the White, whom Tristram marries because she is like Isolde of Ireland.

> **Isolde**
> Alternative spellings: Ysolde, Iseult.

Kay

Sir Kay is King Arthur's foster brother. He is often portrayed as a mischievous, rude and doubting knight.

Lady of the Lake

The Lady of the Lake is the mysterious woman who gives Arthur Excalibur. She is also said to have schooled Sir Lancelot.

There are differences in various stories. In Malory's version she is killed by Balin, who is then banished and told to redeem himself. Yet, at the end, she is one of the Ladies of Avalon who can heal King Arthur after he has received his wound and is taken to Avalon.

Lamorak

Sir Lamorak is one of the sons of King Pellinore, according to Sir Thomas Malory. He becomes one of the mightiest of knights. When his father King Pellinore is killed by Sir Gawain (for Pellinore had killed Sir Gawain's father, King Lot) he does not seek vengeance. Later, however, he is discovered in Queen Morgawse's bed and is later ambushed by Sir Gawain and his brothers, Sir Gaheris and Sir Agravaine. Their other brother, Sir Gareth, refuses to be involved in such a dishonourable act.

Lancelot

Sir Lancelot du Lac is the greatest of the knights throughout the Arthurian saga, until he falls in love with Queen Guinevere. His desire for her prevents him from being worthy enough to achieve the Grail. Instead, his son, Galahad, does so.

Lancelot was also originally called Galahad. He was apparently brought up by the Lady of the Lake.

> *Sir Lancelot*
> Alternative spelling: Launcelot.

Leodegraunce

King Leodegraunce, the ruler of Caemelarde, is the father of Guinevere.

Lionel

Sir Lionel is the brother of Sir Bors and cousin to Sir Lancelot. In the Quest for the Holy Grail he is bewitched and filled with anger that Sir Bors, his brother, does not save him. Under the madness that is on him he slays a monk and is then told that he must do penance, while Sir Bors must continue on the quest.

Lucan

Sir Lucan is one of King Arthur's true knights. He is one of three left standing on Arthur's side at the final battle, including King Arthur himself. He helps Bedivere carry the wounded King from the field after he slays Mordred, but he has a fearsome abdominal wound from which his bowels start to fall out, and he dies in front of Arthur.

Lynette

Lady Lynette is a damsel who leads Sir Gareth on a quest whereby he has to defeat a green, red, blue and black knight, in order to rescue the Lady Lyones.

> *Lady Lynette*
> Alternative spellings: Linet, Lynet.

Lyones

Lady Lyones is rescued by Sir Gareth in the tale of Gareth and Lynette. There are two endings. Malory has Gareth and Lady Lyones falling in love and marrying, while Tennyson has Lady Lynette nursing the wounded Sir Gareth and marrying him.

Mark

Mark is king of Cornwall and the uncle of Sir Tristram.

Manessen

Sir Manessen is an adulterous knight who is a cousin of Sir Accolon. He has been captured by the knight that he had cuckolded and is in danger of being drowned. Morgan le Fay has him released and he drowns the other knight.

King Mark of Cornwall, by Howard Pyle, 1905.

Meliodas

King Meliodas of Lyoness is Tristram's father. He is married to Elizabeth.

Melliagraunce

Sir Melliagraunce is the knight who kidnaps Queen Guinevere after she sends Sir Lancelot away. He returns and rescues her but Sir Melliagraunce then deviously captures Lancelot and imprisons him in his dungeon. Lancelot escapes, thanks to another damsel who falls in love with him.

Merlin

The great wizard is first referred to by Geoffrey of Monmouth in *Historia Regum Britanniae*, or the *History of the Kings of Britain*, written in 1135. It is thought that he may have based his character upon *Myrddin Wyllt* or

Merlin Caledonensis, a Sixth Century prophet and supposed madman. He is mentioned in the *Annales Cambriae* written in the Ninth Century.

Nennius, in his *Historia Brittonum* or *History of the Britons*, written about 830 AD, describes the story of King Vortigern who invited the Saxons to Britain in exchange for the hand of Hengist's daughter. It is retold by the Jersey-born poet Wace in his Twelfth Century work, *Roman de Brut*.

Vortigern is advised to build a tower near to Mount Snowdon and to sanctify it with the blood of a boy that has no father. Attempts to build one had previously resulted in the building materials disappearing. A boy called Ambrosius is found who argues with the wise men, and tells them that under the ground there is a pool and within the pool there are two buried serpents or dragons which are the cause of the problem. One dragon is red and is Vortigern's dragon and the other dragon is white and represents the Saxons. They would do battle and a final battle would bring victory to the Britons.

Geoffrey of Monmouth embellishes this tale and identifies the boy as Merlin, suggesting that his other name was Ambrosius.

Merlin is the great mover of events. In some versions he creates the Round Table. He is certainly responsible for the magically appearing names on the Sieges.

Malory introduces him right at the start when Sir Ulfius, counsellor to Uther Pendragon, seeks him out and then Merlin arranges by magic for Uther to seduce Igrayne, the wife of Gorlois, Duke of Cornwall. The result of their union is Arthur, whom Merlin takes away in secret and places with Sir Ector, who will be his foster father. He arranges for the sword in the stone that shows that Arthur is the rightful king and he leads Arthur to the lake where he receives

Illumination of a Fifteenth Century manuscript of *Historia Regum Britanniae* showing King of the Britons Vortigern and Ambros watching the fight between two dragons. Unknown artist.

Excalibur. He advises him on what to do in his early reign, making many prophesies, not all of which Arthur takes in or recalls.

T.H. White uses Merlin as a major character in his first book *The Sword in the Stone*, in which he teaches the young boy Wart. In his final book *The Book of Merlyn*, published posthumously, he has Merlin return on the eve of the Battle of Camlann to complete his spiritual education.

Mark Twain creates quite a different Merlin in his book *A Connecticut Yankee at the Court of King Arthur*. In this he is a devious charlatan who is exposed by the time-travelling American.

Merlin is the blueprint for the wizards of all the tales that followed the Arthurian saga.

Mordred

Sir Mordred is the incestuously conceived son of Arthur and his half-sister, Morgawse. Merlin tells Arthur that a child born in May will bring about his death and the destruction of all that he holds dear. Arthur then commits a black deed. He orders that sons born in May of any of his lords should be surrendered. They are then put aboard a ship and cast adrift. The ship is wrecked but Mordred is saved and is brought up by a good knight. He is presented at court when he is fourteen and made a Knight of the Round Table. There is thus a bad apple in the crop of the finest knights. The fact that he was born through incest and of a duplicitous mother clearly indicates in the Romances that Mordred has to be ultimately evil. Yet Arthur is by no means blameless in all of this. Mordred and Agravaine plot to expose Guinevere and Sir Lancelot's adultery, setting the chain of events that will lead to the total ruin of all that Arthur holds dear.

When King Arthur goes to wage war against Sir Lancelot in France, Mordred is left to rule the land. He lets it be known that Arthur is dead and has himself proclaimed king. He tries to foist himself on Guinevere who secures herself in the Tower of London. King Arthur returns and they fight at Dover, where Sir Gawain is killed. Then they meet at Camlann where a great battle is fought until only King Arthur, Sir Bedivere and Sir Mordred are left alive. King Arthur impales Mordred on Ron, his spear, but Mordred drags himself along the spear and deals Arthur a mortal blow to the head.

Mordred dies in great agony while King Arthur slumps slowly and quietly to the ground.

> **Sir Mordred**
>
> Alternative spelling: Modred.

Morgawse

One of the three daughters of Gorlois and Igrayne, Morgawse is sister to Elaine and Morgan le Fay. She marries King Lot of Orkney and they have five sons – Gawain, Agravaine, Gaheris and Gareth – and Mordred, who has actually been conceived incestuously with King Arthur.

Morgan le Fay

One of the three daughters of Gorlois and Igrayne, Morgan le Fay is sister to Elaine and Morgawse. She is sent to a nunnery where she is schooled in magic and becomes a great sorceress, the mortal enemy of King Arthur. Much that goes wrong in Arthur's realm is due to her.

She marries King Urien of Gore and has a son, Sir Uwaine. She is lover to Sir Accolon, to whom she gives Excalibur when she plans to have both Urien and Arthur killed. She and Accolon would then rule as king and queen.

At the end of the saga, however, she again becomes one of the Ladies of Avalon and receives Arthur's wounded body. Seemingly they have reconciled their lifelong enmity.

Naciens

Naciens is a hermit who appears several times in the tale, especially in the Quest for the Holy Grail, for he is the Priest of the Holy Grail. In a way he is like Merlin, but whereas Merlin is clearly a wizard, Naciens is a man touched by the divine.

Oringle

Sir Oringle of Limors is the knight who tries to seduce Enid when she and Sir Geraint rest at his castle overnight after Geraint has defeated and killed eighteen knights. Geraint is overcome by sheer numbers when he is confronted by Sir Oringle and his eighty knights and is knocked unconscious. It is thought that he is dead, but later at the sound of Enid's voice he awakes and slays Sir Oringle.

Outlake

Sir Outlake is a good knight, the rightful owner of the castle which has been stolen from him by his brother, the cowardly Sir Danas. King Arthur is duped into fighting him or his champion by Morgan le Fay's evil scheme. Since Sir Outlake had previously been wounded, Sir Accolon fights on his behalf.

Pelles

King Pelles, the Maimed King or the Fisher King. (See Fisher King). His daughter is Lady Elaine who induces Sir Lancelot to sleep with her, conceiving Galahad as a result. Pelles is, therefore, the grandfather of Sir Galahad.

Pellinore

King Pellinore of the Isles, possibly Anglesey, has a lifelong hunt for the Questing Beast. He defeats Arthur in combat but later saves him and kills King Lot. This act gains the hatred and ill will of Sir Gawain and his brothers. Later, Sir Gawain kills King Pellinore.

In some tales, King Pellinore is the father of Percival, in others, Percival's father is unknown. It is even suggested that it could be Sir Gawain.

Perarde

Sir Perade is the Knight of the Black Lands in the tale of Gareth and Lynette.

Percival

Sir Percival is one of the three Grail Knights, along with Sir Bors and Sir Galahad. He is brought up by his mother in the wilds of Wales without seeing another human being until he sees Sir Lancelot. Determined to be a knight, he goes to King Arthur's court and proves himself.

Some accounts have King Pellinore as his father, while Roger Lancelyn Green suggests that his father is Sir Gawain and his mother is Lady Ragnell. His sister is one of the Grail maidens and she sacrifices herself on the quest for the Holy Grail by bleeding to death.

After the Grail is achieved, he takes holy orders and devotes himself to serving and praying to God.

Sir Percival

Alternative spelling: Parsifal.

Pertolope

Sir Pertolope is the Knight of the Green Lands in the tale of Gareth and Lynette.

Perymones

Sir Perymones is the Knight of the Blue Lands in the tale of Gareth and Lynette.

Ragnell

Dame Ragnell, or Lady Ragnell, is a beautiful lady who has had a spell placed upon her that turns her into a loathsome hag. She saves King Arthur from Sir Gromer Somer Joure who has posed the king a riddle. Her price is to wed a knight that very day. Sir Gawain marries her and breaks half the curse so that she is beautiful half the day. She tells him that he must choose which half of the day he would like her to be ugly, and which beautiful. He tells her the choice is hers and the spell is completely broken so she can be beautiful all the time. They have seven years of happiness and then she disappears – possibly to have a child, Percival, whom she brings up on her own in the wilds of Wales.

Ryan

King Ryan of North Wales. He demands tribute from King Arthur and is defeated by Balin.

Tarquyn

Sir Tarquyn is a huge knight who defeats many Knights of the Round Table because he has vowed revenge upon Sir Lancelot, who slew his brother, Sir Carados.

How Sir Tarquine bare Sir Ector clean out of his Saddle, by Alfred Kappes, 1881.

> ### Sir Tarquyn
> Alternative spellings: Tarquin, Tarquine.

Tor

Sir Tor is one of the sons of King Pellinore. He is involved in the quest to save the bracket.

Tristram

Sir Tristram of Lyonesse is the nephew of King Mark of Cornwall. He is sent to Ireland and falls in love with Isolde of Ireland. Their love is intensified forever when they both unwittingly take a love potion on a ship back to England. He marries another Isolde, Isolde the White, and lies dying after receiving a poisoned wound in a fight. He arranges a secret message with Isolde of Ireland so that, if she will come to save him with her healing ability, a white sail shall be flown. When the ship is sighted, he asks Isolde the White what colour the sail is and she, knowing about the message, says it is black. Tristram then dies of a broken heart.

> ### Sir Tristram
> Alternative spelling: Tristan.

Ulfius

Sir Ulfius is Uther Pendragon's counsellor.

Urien

King Urien of Gore is the husband of Morgan le Fay.

Urry

Sir Urry is a wounded knight who is brought to Camelot and is cured by Sir Lancelot in the tale of *The Passing of King Arthur*.

Uther

King Uther Pendragon is the father of Arthur.

Uwaine

Sir Uwaine is the cousin of Sir Gawain and the son of Morgan le Fay.

> ### Sir Uwaine
> Alternative spelling: Yvaine.

Viviene

The sorceress Viviene in some versions of the tales. She is one of the Ladies of Avalon, and is sometimes identified as the Lady of the Lake. She is taught by Merlin and eventually induces him to go to a cave under a rock where he falls into an eternal, mystical sleep.

Viviene

Alternative spellings: Vivien, Vivian, Nimue, Nineve, Nyneve.

Vortigern

King Vortigern rules Powys and is regarded as a tyrant. He invites the Saxons to come to help him fight the Picts, taking Hengist's daughter in marriage. He is said to be building a tower or a stronghold and is advised to sprinkle the area with the blood of a boy who has no father. Merlin is the boy who reveals that two buried serpents have cursed the area.

What notable objects and buildings are discovered in the Arthurian stories?

Some of the objects that are included here are very important, such as the Round Table and Excalibur, Arthur's wonderful sword. Yet there are other smaller things that are also worthy of note.

Carbonek

This is the Grail Castle where the Grail Procession is seen. It is a mystical castle that appears and disappears, located in the heart of the Waste Lands. King Pelles, the Fisher King, rules the Waste Lands and cannot leave his castle.

Castle Terrabyl

This is one of two castles owned by Gorlois, Duke of Cornwall. When Uther Pendragon makes war on him, Gorlois secures his wife, Igrayne, in Castle Tintagel and himself in Castle Terrabyl where he is killed.

Castle Joyous Gard

This is Sir Lancelot's main castle. There are two possible sites for it. One is Alnwick Castle and the other is Bamborough Castle, both in Northumberland.

Dolorous Stroke

The Dolorous Stroke is the stabbing of King Pelles by Balin. Either the Spear of Longinus is used or the Dolorous Sword. The point is that King Pelles, also known as the Fisher King, cannot be healed except by blood from the spear, collected in the Holy Grail.

Excalibur

King Arthur's sword, said to have been forged in Avalon and given to Arthur by The Lady of the Lake. It is a mighty sword that none can resist.

Excalibur's scabbard, which would give Arthur invulnerability, is stolen by his sister Morgan le Fay and cast into the lake so that it will never be found again.

It is not to be confused with the sword in the stone, which is another sword whose purpose was simply to determine the rightful king.

Gringalet

Sir Gawain's mighty steed.

Ron

This is King Arthur's spear. It does not itself seem to have any magical feature, as does Gungnir, the spear of Odin in Norse mythology, which had been forged by the dwarves and could never be deflected and never missed its mark. Odin (or Wodin) was the chief of the gods and was venerated by the Angles and Saxons who invaded Britain in the Fifth and Sixth Centuries.

At the final battle King Arthur kills Sir Mordred with Ron. Mordred, realising that he has a mortal wound, drags himself along the shaft of the spear to reach Arthur and deal him a fatal blow.

Spear or Lance?

This is an interesting question, since the popular image of the Knights of the Round Table has them suited in full armour – which is actually more in keeping with the Fourteenth and Fifteenth Centuries than the Sixth – charging at an opponent with a huge lance outstretched before them.

In fact if we are to put Arthur in the context of the Sixth Century then his weapon would almost certainly have been a spear, which would have been the logical and practical weapon for a man on horseback. The lance was a longer adaptation of the spear which was used in warfare by cavalry.

The jousting lance was a later development for the special jousting tournaments that developed in Europe in the late Middle Ages as an organised competition as opposed to the melees that preceded them.

The Holy Grail

Also known as *the Sangreal*, the legend is that this was the drinking vessel used by Jesus Christ at the Last Supper. It is also thought to have been used to collect his blood when he was crucified.

Joseph of Arimathea is said to have brought the Grail to Britain from the Holy Land. Robert de Boron seems to have been the first writer to refer to it in his work *Joseph d'Arimathie.*

Chrétien de Troyes refers to it as being more like a salver.

The quest for the Holy Grail assumes great importance in the Arthurian saga, for it will allow for the Messiah-like figure of Sir Galahad to ascend to heaven, cure the Maimed King, Pelles (also known as the Fisher King) and bring hope and healing to the Waste Lands.

The Questing Beast

This is a creature that is named in different versions of the tale. In early versions it is a small creature like a fox, but in Malory's *Le Morte d'Arthur* and in T.H. White's *The Once and Future King* it is a real chimera. It had an unholy birth, possibly from the conception of a child by the shape-shifting devil.

In this version, which is in keeping with the legends as illustrated in this book, it has the head of a serpent, the body of a leopard, the hindquarters of a lion and the feet of a hare. It is not easy to find, of course, and the quest is partly the hunt for it, but also the braying noise that it makes, as if it has forty braying or questing dogs in its stomach.

King Pellinore takes up the lifelong quest for the beast.

The Round Table

The Round Table was first introduced into the Arthur story by the Jersey poet Wace, in his work *Roman de Brut*, sometime in the mid-Twelfth Century. It is really a brilliant feature of the story because it makes the fellowship of knights that King Arthur introduces both plausible and elite.

In some versions, particularly Malory's *Le Morte d'Arthur*, it is a gift from King Leodegraunce, Guinevere's father, and in others Merlin creates it.

The point of the Round Table was that it had no head, so everyone was an equal. King Arthur would, of course, sit on his throne so although it was supposed to be an elite fellowship, yet some were more elite than others. This is brought home when the chairs or 'Sieges' are each allocated to the individual knights. The Siege Perilous, which was first introduced in the Vulgate Cycle, is reserved for the Grail Knight, Sir Galahad. In some versions of the tale it is Sir Percival who is the Grail Knight and he sits in it. It is fatal for any other to sit in it.

There is considerable variation in the number of knights that could sit at the Round Table. Robert de Boron says that it sat fifty knights whereas

Layamon, who adapted Wace's work, said that it could seat 1,600 knights. Other quotes suggest 450 knights, but the logistics of this would be hard to imagine since that would be a colossal table. The Round Table that hangs in Winchester Great Hall weighs over a ton, is eighteen feet in diameter and used to have twelve legs. Believed to have been made during the reign of Edward I (1239-1307), it was painted during the reign of Henry VIII and rather resembles a dart board. There is a Tudor Rose at its centre and a portrait of King Henry at King Arthur's place at the table. It would have enough room to seat a king and twenty-four knights.

The Round Table in Winchester Great Hall.

The noble order that might have been

In 1344 King Edward III was inspired to create a noble order of knights based upon King Arthur and his Knights of the Round Table. He held a massive joust at Windsor Castle and apparently considered calling the new order of nobility the Order of the Round Table, re-establishing all of the knightly qualities of the fellowship of the original Round Table. He foresaw having a complement of three hundred knights and began construction of a great circular building, measuring two hundred feet across, in the upper ward of Windsor Castle. The outbreak of war with France interrupted building and the plans were modified for another purpose in 1348. The Order of the Round Table was also modified and instead he created the Order of the Garter.

The sword in the stone

This is a sword implanted by Merlin in an anvil a-top a stone. It is first mentioned by Robert de Boron and is later used by Sir Thomas Malory as a means to show that only the true and rightful king can draw it. The sword was meant to signify justice and the stone the rock of Christianity. By drawing it from the stone Arthur would symbolically be able to dispense justice in the name of Christianity.

It provided the name for the first of T.H. White's books in his Arthurian pentalogy.

The Waste Lands

The Dolorous Stroke results in three lands being laid to waste, hence the Waste Lands. They can only be restored by the blood of Christ and the coming of the Holy Grail. This is the whole purpose of the tale of the Holy Grail.

Where are the places named in the Arthurian stories?

Arthurian scholars have tried to chart Arthur's realm according to the places named in the various sources. It is not an easy matter for they too often have different names. Also, the way in which various knights head off on a quest and, after passing through a forest seem mystically to cover hundreds of miles on their charger in a very short time, makes it impossible to realistically pinpoint places with any certainty.

Places like Tintagel, London and Caerleon are quite clear. They are actual places that anyone can visit. Other places such as Badon Mount, the Plain of Camlann and Camelot itself have tantalised historians, archaeologists and Arthurian enthusiasts for years. Some authors are convinced that they can, and in some cases have, been located.

It is not the purpose of this book to try to persuade the reader about the veracity of a historic Arthur, or to prove the links between a site and the Arthurian saga. In this section, I shall merely describe several sites that the interested reader may like to visit.

Who, What, Where and When in Arthur's Realm

Arthur's Seat

This mountain overlooking Holyrood in Edinburgh has an extremely doubtful connection with King Arthur, yet it has been linked with him since the Fifteenth Century.

Arthur's Stone

This is a Neolithic chambered tomb seven miles east of Hay-on-Wye in Herefordshire, which is looked after by English Heritage. Legend has it that King Arthur fought and slew a giant here. As the giant fell, he left the indentation of his elbows in the stones.

Camelot

> *At the end of an hour we saw a far-away town sleeping in a valley by a winding river; and beyond it on a hill, a vast grey fortress, with towers and turrets, the first I had ever seen out of a picture.*
> *"Bridgeport?" said I, pointing.*
> *"Camelot," said he.*
> A Connecticut Yankee at the Court
> of King Arthur, *Mark Twain*

Mark Twain's novel about an American who finds himself transported back to the days of King Arthur is a classic piece of fiction. Where exactly Camelot was, if it existed at all, we do not know. Mark Twain certainly didn't know but he created a place that the reader wanted to visit.

Chrétien de Troyes, the Twelfth Century poet, is the first person to mention King Arthur's court at Camelot in his poem *Lancelot*. Tennyson mentions it as 'many tower'd Camelot' in *The Lady of Shalott*. It is this fine image that is used again and again in television and film recreation.

There are, of course several places that have been identified as possible sites for Camelot:

Winchester

Sir Thomas Malory identifies Camelot as Winchester. In Winchester Great Hall near the Cathedral there hangs a Round Table. It is plausible as a site, since it was the capital of Wessex in King Alfred the Great's day.

Cadbury Castle

The antiquarian John Leland identified Cadbury Castle in Somerset as the site of Camelot. It is an Iron Age hill fort which was excavated between 1966 and 1970 by Leslie Alcott and his team of archaeologists. The dig was referred to as Cadbury-Camelot. Although it revealed many exquisite artifacts, and showed that it was a hill fort that had been refortified, Alcott's conclusion was that it was too late a site to claim to be Camelot. Thus the name reverted simply to Cadbury Castle hill fort. It is appealing in terms of being close to the River Cam.

Camulodunum

This was the Roman name for the town of Colchester in Essex. What goes against it is the fact that it would have been well inside Saxon territory.

Camelford

A village in Cornwall, Camelford has for a long time had a claim since it is near the River Camel. Readers of Geoffrey of Monmouth might imagine that this could be linked with Camlann.

Caerleon

Caerleon is certainly associated with King Arthur, leading many to speculate as to whether it could have been Camelot. Yet Geoffrey of Monmouth describes it quite clearly as itself, and Sir Thomas Malory talks about it as a place. There is no reason to suppose that it would be Camelot and not just itself, Caerleon. It does still have the outlines of a Roman amphitheatre, which could possibly relate to the Round Table.

Roman amphitheatre at Caerleon, Wales, UK. Photo by John Lamper.

Chester

Chester is a leading contender. Indeed, Christopher Gidlow gives a compelling argument in his 2010 book, *Revealing King Arthur: Swords, Stones and Digging for Camelot,* that Chester was the 'City of the Legions'

Roman Amphitheatre – Actors at the Roman Amphitheatre in Chester, Photograph by Gerald England.

that is mentioned by the Ninth Century writer, Nennius. The Chester Roman amphitheatre could conceivably have been where King Arthur held his court and the Round Table may have been a fanciful name given to it, wherein the court could have assembled.

Camlann

The location of the great battle of Camlann, where King Arthur is supposed to have received his mortal wound from his son, Sir Mordred, is equally steeped in mystery. The *Annales Cambriae* date it to 537 AD.

There are several contending sites:

- Queen Camel in Somerset, near to the River Cam and the hill fort of Cadbury
- Castlesteads, a Roman fort on Hadrian's Wall in Cumbria, which was called Camboglanna
- Camelford, a village in Cornwall near the River Camel; Geoffrey of Monmouth implies that Camlann was near the river
- Camelon, near Falkirk; (see Chapter Nine on The Real Arthur and the section on *Artur Mac Aidan*)
- T.H. White suggests that Camlann was fought on Salisbury Plain near Stonehenge

Dover

This great port city in Kent with its castle was said to be the site of a great battle fought between the armies of King Arthur and Sir Mordred, during which Sir Gawain was killed.

Glastonbury

This delightful town in Somerset is said by some to be the site for Avalon, since during the Fifth and Sixth Centuries, Glastonbury Tor would have been surrounded by marshland that could often have been flooded and covered in mist.

The origins of Glastonbury are obscure, but legend has it that it was established as a religious site by Joseph of Arimathea in the First Century.

That may be quite fanciful but it is one of the deeply rooted associations that have grown up around it.

The actual Abbey was established in the Seventh Century, and rebuilding in the Tenth Century made it a major religious centre.

In 1184, there was a fire which destroyed much of the building. Rebuilding began almost immediately. In 1191 a grave was discovered in the cemetery between two pyramids when the monks were digging a new grave for one of their number. According to Gerald of Wales, a chronicler who visited shortly afterwards, they found deep down a large hollowed oak, containing the bodies of a large man and a smaller woman. Long blonde hair was still present with the woman's body. Under the coffin (different accounts say that there were two separate coffins, the man's underneath the woman's) they found a slab with a leaden cross, on which was written, 'Here lies buried the famous King Arthur with Guinevere his second wife in the Isle of Avalon.'

The grave is still there for all to visit.

This is of course quite compelling evidence, yet it has been regarded by many historians as merely a hoax perpetrated by the monks in 1191, perhaps to raise money to help with their rebuilding. If Glastonbury could be regarded as a pilgrimage site, then they could tap into that as a source of revenue.

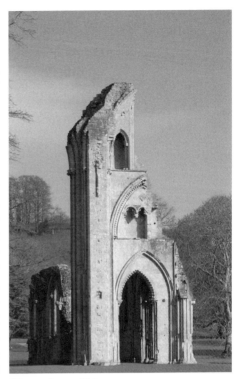

Glastonbury Abbey.

The site of King Arthur's tomb.

Christopher Gidlow, a renowned Arthurian scholar and lifelong enthusiast for the Middle Ages and the Arthurian legends has written two excellent books on Arthur, *The Reign of Arthur* (2004) and *Revealing King Arthur: Swords, Stones and Digging for Camelot* (2010). He considers whether the monks or even King Henry II would have had anything to gain by perpetrating or condoning such a hoax, and comes

Glastonbury Tor.

to the conclusion that they would not. Indeed, there is no reason why the graves should not be those of Arthur and his queen. The main stumbling block is the leaden cross which would not have belonged to the Sixth Century.

Logres

This is the name used to refer to Arthur's realm. Its origin is uncertain but, loosely, it means England.

London

The capital city of England needs no introduction today. It was a thriving centre in Roman times. Layamon mentions London several times, suggesting that at times King Arthur moved his court there.

Sir Thomas Malory has Queen Guinevere secure herself inside the Tower of London in order to evade the attentions of Sir Mordred.

Lud's Church

A natural fissure in the rocks in Staffordshire, this is a proposed site for the Green Chapel in *Sir Gawain and the Green Knight*.

Lyoness

Lyoness was a land said to border with Cornwall but which is no more. It was said to have fallen into the sea after the days of Arthur.

It is possibly located somewhere around the Scilly Isles.

Merlin's Cave

Under the rocks of Tintagel is the famous cave where Merlin is said to have plucked the infant Arthur from the waves.

Merlin's Cave, Tintagel, Cornwall. Looking down from Barras Nose to one end of Merlin's Cave and Tintagel Beach, which is only accessible at low tide. Photograph by Janet Richardson.

Merlin's Hill

If you travel two miles east of Carmarthen in Wales along the A40 you will find Bryn Myrddin, or Merlin's Hill. Its summit resembles a chair and it is said by Gerald of Wales to have been the place where Merlin was trapped in eternal sleep.

Merlin's Mound

This is also known as Merlin's Barrow and Marlborough Mound. It is a stepped hill in the grounds of Marlborough College. This is an English public school in Wiltshire (which does not mean that it is open to the public). The school would need to be contacted before venturing to see this, one of the sites where Merlin is supposedly sleeping, since being tricked and magically imprisoned by Viviene.

Mount Badon

The great Battle of Mount Badon (or Mons Badonicus), one of the decisive victories that Arthur is said to have had against the Saxons, was an important event in British history but it cannot be precisely dated, nor placed. It is thought to have occurred sometime between 490 and 520 AD.

There are several contending sites:

- Liddington Castle, above the village of Badbury near Swindon in Wiltshire

- Badbury Hill Fort in Dorset
- Solsbury Hill, near Bath
- Buxton in Derbyshire
- Bardon Hill in Leicestershire

Pendragon Castle

This is a ruin in Mallerstang Dale in Cumbria which is reputed to have belonged to King Uther Pendragon. He is said to have attempted to divert the River Eden that it looks down on in order to fill a moat around the castle.

The Pillar of Eliseg

In a field overlooking the ruins of Valle Crucis Abbey, a few miles from Llangollen in Clwyd on the way to the Horseshoe Pass, there is a standing pillar cross which bears a weathered inscription. It was erected by Cyngen, Prince of Powys in honour of his great-grandfather, Eliseg. It was broken by Cromwell's troops during the English Civil War, so that when it was re-erected it was merely a pillar. Nevertheless, it has given its name to the area and the Abbey, as 'Valley of the Cross'. It now stands atop a burial mound which was excavated in 1779, and which is currently being investigated. Archaeologists from Bangor and Chester universities started excavating in 2010 and Bronze Age finds have been discovered.

The significance of the pillar is that its inscriptions are said to have related to a genealogy and mentioned Vortigern.

Samson

A small isle in the Isles of Scilly, this is reputedly where Sir Tristram fought and killed Sir Morholt.

Stonehenge

This is the greatest henge in Europe, which stands on Salisbury Plain. Geoffrey of Monmouth describes it as a monument erected by Merlin to honour the warriors who fell in a great battle.

T.H. White places the last great battle of Camlann upon Salisbury Plain.

Tintagel

An impressive place on the North Cornwall coast, Tintagel is reputed to be the birth place of Arthur.

Tintagel island is reached by a narrow strip of land from the mainland. When the Atlantic winds blow it is as exposed a site as one could ever imagine.

Tintagel Castle.

At one time it was thought to have been an early monastery but excavations reveal that it is likely to have been a Roman trading centre, for all manner of exotic Mediterranean pottery from the Fourth and Fifth Centuries have been found there. Glass has also been found. From our point of view, a fascinating find was discovered when a team of archaeologists led by Professor Chris Morris from the University of Glasgow discovered a piece of slate that is at least 1,500 years old. It bears a Latin inscription that may refer to Arthur. It is known as the 'Arthur Stone' (see Chapter Nine on The Real Arthur).

A later medieval castle was built in 1233 for Reginald, Earl of Cornwall. It must have been a magnificent building whose ruins excite the imagination of every passing Arthurian enthusiast.

Geoffrey of Monmouth relates that Gorlois, Duke of Cornwall left Igrayne at Tintagel while he did battle with Uther Pendragon, but Merlin arranged through his magic for Uther to visit her in the castle disguised as Gorlois. Arthur was conceived as a result. This is interesting, since it may have been part of a propaganda ploy to link the Norman landowners with 'earlier' rulers in order to establish a pedigree. The brother of Reginald, Earl of Cornwall was Robert, Earl of Gloucester, who just happened to be Geoffrey's patron.

Sir Thomas Malory tells the tale of Tristram and Isolde and begins it at Tintagel, which is owned by King Mark of Cornwall.

Tristram's Stone

On the roadside between Fowey and Castle Dore in Cornwall there is a seven foot standing stone which is said to have marked the grave of Sir Tristram. Upon it is inscribed in Latin:

DRUSTANS HIC IACIT CVNOWORI
FILVS

It means, *'Drustans here lies, of Cunomorus the son'* and is thought to refer to Tristram and King Mark.

The Tristan Stone, by the A308, Fowey. Photograph by Rod Allday.

Plaque detailing the history of the Tristan Stone. Photograph by Rod Allday.

The Vitalinus Stone

In the old kingdom of Dyfed, which is now northern Pembrokeshire in Wales, there is a small village called Nevern. In the churchyard of St Brynach there are several Fifth and Sixth Century stones, possibly marking graves. One of them is inscribed with both Latin and Ogham script. (Ogham is an ancient alphabetical system consisting of notches; it is found on ancient stones, possibly representing a Celtic language. It is said to be named after Ogma, the god of eloquence.) Known as the Vitalinus Stone, it is thought that it could mark the burial site of King Vortigern.

The Vitalinus Stone, Nevern. Nevern may have been the final resting place for Vortigern. Photograph by Cered.

When did various tales take place?

There are a series of mini-questions to be considered here. In which year or years did certain things take place? Well, it has to be said that apart from events like the Battle of Mount Badon and the Battle of Camlann, the dates of which are highly speculative, we cannot date any of the tales to any year, apart from the coming of Galahad to take his Siege Perilous, which Malory dates to 454 years after the Passion of Christ.

If we look at a tale such as *Sir Gawain and the Green Knight*, we are unlikely to be able to date it is an event, since it is clearly a poem that was first told in the late Fourteenth Century. The best that we can do is to try to assess at which time of the year certain tales were set.

Most of the tales relate to various events in the Church calendar when the Knights of the Round Table would meet to celebrate some feast or another. These we can date a little more precisely within the years.

Christmas

This is the day to celebrate the birth of Jesus and is generally held on the 25th of December. The choice of this date was apparently worked

The Middle Ages

This is a large time period that begins in about the Fifth Century and ends in the Fifteenth Century. It extends from the fall of the Western Roman Empire in 476 AD until the start of the modern era in the Fifteenth Century. It is divided up roughly as follows:

- Early Middle Ages – from Fifth Century to circa 1000 AD (or 1066, the Battle of Hastings and Norman Conquest)
- High Middle Ages – from circa 1000 to 1300 (or the time of the Crusades)
- Late Middle Ages – from 1300 to 1485 (the time of famines and calamities with 95 famines in Britain, the Hundred Years War and the Wars of the Roses culminating in the Battle of Bosworth Field, the end of the House of York and the beginning of the Tudor period)

out from the reported time of Mary's conception, which was during Elizabeth's sixth month of pregnancy with John the Baptist. The great genius Isaac Newton argued that the 25th of December was chosen to correspond with the winter solstice.

In the Arthurian tales the following events begin at Christmas:

- Merlin calls the lords together for a meeting on Christmas Day and while they are at mass the sword in the stone appears
- The Green Knight comes to Camelot on New Year's Day
- At Carlisle, King Arthur is goaded into a quest which results in Sir Gawain marrying the loathsome Dame Ragnell

The Feast of Candlemas

This occurred on the 2nd of February. It was to commemorate two things:

- The presentation of the child Jesus at the Temple of Jerusalem
- The Virgin Mary's purification

A candle procession would take place before mass. This was said to celebrate the forty day period of purification after giving childbirth (when women were not permitted to enter a temple) when Mary took Jesus to the Temple at Jerusalem. In the New Testament the Gospel of Luke relates that Anna and Simeon hold the child and Simeon declares that he will be 'a light to the world.' Thus the occasion was called Candlemas and it became the day when all of the candles in the church were blessed for the year.

In *The Coming of Arthur*, the decision about who should be king is put off until Candlemas, since the lords cannot accept the boy Arthur as their king.

The Feast of Easter

This is the central date in the Church calendar. Jesus Christ was crucified on Good Friday. He is said to have risen again three days later, and this resurrection is commemorated on Easter Day or Easter Sunday. It is not known precisely which year his death and resurrection occurred but it has been estimated to have happened sometime around 30 AD.

Easter marks the end of Lent, a forty day period of fasting, praying and doing penance.

Easter is a moveable feast, so its timing varies year by year. It was determined by the First Council of Nicaea, a meeting of bishops under the Roman Emperor Constantine, that it should be celebrated on the Sunday after the first full moon that occurred after the vernal (or spring) equinox.

Eastertide is the period of time between Easter and Pentecost.

- In *The Coming of Arthur*, the decision about who should be king is put off a second time until Easter
- The young Percival presents himself at Caerleon
- In *The Tale of Sir Lancelot and Elaine*, a hermit comes to Camelot and prophesies that the Siege Perilous will one day be filled by Sir Galahad
- In *The Tale of Geraint and Enid*, the young Geraint presents himself at Caerleon and tells King Arthur of the white stag with golden horns; he accompanies Queen Guinevere and one of her ladies and sets off in pursuit of the Black Knight

The Feast of Pentecost

This date is frequently mentioned in the *Tales of King Arthur*, because it was regarded as a significant date in the religious year. It is mentioned in the Acts of the Apostles and commemorates the descent of the Holy Spirit upon the twelve apostles after the resurrection of Christ.

It takes place seven weeks after Easter and is regarded as the birth of the Church. Its importance to King Arthur establishes a link between Christendom and the chivalric basis of King Arthur's Camelot.

- In *The Coming of Arthur*, the people demand that the lords accept Arthur as their king; he is crowned first knight and King of England
- Gawain, King Lot's son and Tor, King Pellinore's son are knighted at Pentecost on the wedding day of King Arthur to Guinevere
- Sir Lancelot of the Lake, Sir Lionel, his cousin and Sir Hector de Maris, his half-brother, are knighted one Pentecost and Sir Lancelot sets off on his first quest some days later
- One Pentecost, Gareth of Orkney comes to Camelot and asks to serve in the kitchen for a year; on the following Pentecost he sets off on a quest with the Lady Lynette
- *The Tale of the Quest for the Holy Grail* begins at Camelot on Pentecost

The Feast of Michaelmas

The feast of St Michael the Archangel is another common time for the Knights of the Round Table to meet up in the legends. St Michael was venerated because he was said to have defeated Lucifer in the war in heaven.

It corresponds with the 29th of September and was regarded by the Church as a Holy Day of Obligation, meaning that people were expected to take mass.

In the legends it was a good time to date the seasons by, since it falls not long after the autumn equinox when the days start to shorten until the shortest day at the winter solstice.

In the tale of *Sir Gawain and the Green Knight* it is a significant time, since the greenery would start to turn colour and fall, indicating that as the leaves died and fell, so too was the possibility of Gawain's death drawing ever closer.

Part Two

King Arthur and the Knights of the Round Table

Myth or fact?

ONCE upon a time there were no doubts in people's minds. King Arthur was regarded as an actual historical character. The King of Britain, the saviour of his people and a true inspiration for all of the monarchs who succeeded him. Yet when historians started to examine the historical record, actually looking for documentary evidence of his rule, it was found that there was very little if any hard evidence.

This very question causes Arthurian scholars, historians, archaeologists and enthusiastic lay researchers to become quite heated. Today there are marked differences in view, from those who aver that the king, his court and his knights were simply characters in various pieces of literature who transcended their literary beginnings, to those who are quite convinced that he was a genuine historical character not far removed from the legends we have just considered in Part One. And, of course, there are various points of view somewhere between those two poles.

In Part Two, we shall look at the literary and historical sources so that you can see where your opinion lies.

Chapter Six

King Arthur as Folklore

Then it was, that magnanimous Arthur, with all the kings and military force of Britain, fought against the Saxons. And though there were many more noble than himself, yet he was twelve times chosen their commander, and it was as often conqueror.

Historia Brittonum (History of the Britons),
Nennius, c.800 AD

THE TITLE of this chapter does not mean that I am putting forward the view that the Arthurian saga is nothing more than a great folk tale. That would be an over-simplification, because there are many strands or threads that form the glorious tapestry that is presented to us. Those threads come from many different disciplines, such as English, Welsh and French literature, medieval poetry, historical texts and archaeology. It clearly cannot be stated categorically that Arthur did not exist, or that if he did, he was a local king, a king of England, a king of Britain or a king of the Britons.

A good place to start is with the question of folklore. Once again it is not because King Arthur should be considered simply as a character in a folk tale, but because there are so many parts of the country which claim to have a link either with Arthur, some of his knights, or with the great wizard, Merlin. These local connections are so diverse geographically as to make it

Chivalry, by Sir Frank Dicksee, 1885.

unlikely that they are all legitimate connections, yet one must ask why they developed such an association in the first place. It may be that they did so because there was a basic need in the local people to believe in some great hero who had saved them and who was sleeping, and could yet arise if needed to help the country again.

What is folklore?

Folklore is the study of the legends, myths, poetry, music, proverbs, popular beliefs and practices of a culture or locality. All cultures have certain stories, beliefs and customs that seem to belong to them and with which individuals in that culture can identify. Stories from the past, often having been kept alive by long oral tradition, are jealously guarded. This may account for the tenacity with which local areas hold on to their claim on certain folk heroes. Robin Hood, for example, is mainly associated with Sherwood Forest and Nottinghamshire but he also has strong links with Wakefield in Yorkshire and even with Robin Hood's Bay on the Yorkshire coast. So, too, with King Arthur who seems to have straddled the country, judging by the places that claim some ownership of his history.

But are folk tales simply fairy tales or are they based on some historical fact? Common sense would tell us that either can be the case.

Archetypal tales

An archetype is a universally understood symbol, meaning or character. The psychologist Carl Jung adapted the term to psychology in about 1919. Essentially, he extensively studied mythology and folk tales and came to the conclusion that there were strong archetypal characters that everyone understood. More than that, he believed that these archetypes played a strong part in fashioning the individual's personality, because one could unconsciously create a 'complex' around a strong archetype in one's life. Thus one's mother, father, teacher could have a huge impact on one's development and also have a bearing in how one saw the world and one's place within it.

Without getting embroiled any further in psychology, it is worth considering how these archetypes occur again and again in myths and folk tales. The eminent Russian scholar Vladimir Propp wrote

Morphology of the Folktale in 1928. It was a seminal study on folklore, in which he described eight archetypal characters that he found in Russian Folk Tales.

- The villain
- The dispatcher who sends the hero on the quest
- The helper – who often has magical powers
- The princess or the prize
- Her father
- The donor or the provider   who gives the hero a magical gift
- The hero
- The false hero

You should already see all of these characters or their equivalents in the Arthurian saga. Each of the tales can throw up several of these archetypes, yet when you put them all together you can see that some of the characters change roles. For the great part of the saga Sir Lancelot, for example, is a hero, yet as we near the end he becomes a false hero. The Lady of the Lake, donor of Excalibur, the magical sword, is not all that she seems and Merlin, the helper, is flawed and blinded by love.

The magical weapons

There are several throughout the saga, most notably:

- Excalibur
- The scabbard of Excalibur
- The sword in the stone – which Arthur removes to become king
- The Dolorous Sword – that Sir Galahad retrieves from the floating block of stone
- The Shield of Joseph of Arimathea
- The Spear of Longinus

The plots found in stories

You may have heard that there are only a limited number of plots in literature. The number varies according to the method of analysis.

Just three

This suggests that everything depends upon the conflict within the story and how it is dealt with.

1. The happy ending – when a character makes a sacrifice for another
2. The unhappy ending – when a sacrifice is not made
3. The literary ending – when the story unfolds backwards, to the inevitable tragedy

We can see all of these in the Arthurian saga of tales.

Or there may be seven

These relate to the characters and the things they interact with.

1. The character against nature
2. The character against the opposite sex
3. The character against the environment
4. The character against a machine or an organisation or army
5. The character against the supernatural
6. The character against him or herself
7. The character against religion

Once again, we can see all of these plots within the framework of the Arthurian sage.

And we could go on

That is right. Ronald Tobias considers there to be twenty plots. Georges Polti considers thirty-six. There is a good chance you would find all of them somewhere within the Arthurian saga.

The point is that the more you can relate to the basic plots and the more archetypes that you can see, the more likely it is that you are looking at a story rather than a historical account.

Well, there is nothing at all wrong with that. Sir Thomas Malory does not pretend to be a historian. He is a re-teller of tales, and an incredibly good one at that.

We always need heroes

Perhaps it is the inherent frailness of being human that makes us revel in tales about strong heroes who can prevail against all odds, who can defeat beasts of incredible strength and who seem to be invulnerable. Every culture produces such tales. The heroes are invariably tagged as being good and honourable, according to what is considered to be good and honourable within that particular society. In a warrior society, then the warrior heroes are gods who can overcome all. They are venerated and people aspire to be like them, to emulate their feats.

Academics and folklorists delve back into the mists of time to find the first heroes. They are often depicted as gods. Witness the pantheons of ancient Egyptian, Roman and Greek gods. The Celtic gods are almost as numerous. Then, when one culture is conquered by another, there seems to be a pattern whereby the old gods and heroes become amalgamated into the new. This happened with the Romans in particular, for they conquered, absorbed the deities of the conquered land and modified them. And it also happened when Christianity swept across Europe. Pagan gods and heroes together with their Roman counterparts seemed to be absorbed as patron saints and local heroes.

Oral tradition, the tales of the campfire and of the great halls kept the stories alive until they were transcribed and embellished. This may have been what happened in the Arthurian saga. As we shall see later in the book when we look at the main contenders for the real historic Arthur, it is no easy matter choosing from any of them. It is obviously such a long time ago and primary sources are few.

Trying to pinpoint who any of the Knights of the Round Table could be based upon is even harder. In their 1992 book *King Arthur: The True Story*, Graham Phillips and Martin Keatman have tried to do this. They conclude that Sir Kay, Sir Bedivere, Morgan le Fay and Guinevere were all based on ancient Celtic deities.

- Sir Kay = Cei
- Sir Bedivere = Bedwyr
- Morgan le Fay = Morrigan
- Guinevere = Gwenhwyfar

They also conclude that Lancelot, Galahad, Percival and Gawain seem to have been characters derived from the French Romances of the Twelfth and Thirteenth Centuries, which were in turn based upon French folk heroes.

Comparative folklore also suggests that the archetypal images of the Holy Grail and the Questing Beast can also be found in older Celtic tales, which talk of the search for a mystical pig and the search for a magic cauldron.

Arthur will come again

There are different versions of the death of Arthur. Some have Arthur being taken to the Isle of Avalon, where he lives still. Other local legends, such as ones from Sewingshields in Northumberland and Alderley Edge in Cheshire, aver that Arthur and his knights are all still sleeping in a mystical cave from which they will rise and defeat the enemy when Albion is threatened.

This image and this legend was fostered in both the World Wars, when it was felt that the people needed to believe in the justness of their cause. If Arthur did not actually rise and appear, yet it was hoped that the national pride and the spirit of Arthur would help the war effort and keep the spirit of the population bolstered.

In a nutshell

One can be over-analytical about the structure of a tale, whether it is a retelling of a historical fact or a folk tale. Let us leave that to the scholars. By all means read the saga and see how many plots and archetypes you can pick out. It seems clear, however, that there are seven really archetypal elements that stand out in the whole saga:

- The rise of a superman hero and his fellow heroes in a time of need
- The quest – in fact, so many of the knight's tales are quests, but the main one is for the Holy Grail
- The love triangle – between Arthur, Guinevere and Sir Lancelot
- The rise and inevitable fall of Camelot and all it stands for
- The fight of good against evil
- The magical weapon, Excalibur
- The mystical Isle of Avalon

Chapter Seven

Literary Sources

And Arthur and his knighthood for a
space
Were all one will, and thro' that strength
the King
Drew in the petty princedoms under him,
Fought, and in twelve great battles over-
came
The heathen hordes, and made a realm
and reign'd.
The Coming of Arthur, Idylls of the King,
Alfred, Lord Tennyson

THE IMAGE that we have of King Arthur is a composite picture from many sources. Nowadays we have television serials, films, videos and video games which give modern Arthurian enthusiasts a clear image of what Camelot and the court of King Arthur might have looked like. I say 'might' because of course we do not really know, given that we do not know whether or not he was a real person or whether there was such a place as Camelot. What we see is the best guess based on the popular image and all of the previous images that have come down to us.

In the Nineteenth Century, before technology provided us with such imagery, people still had a picture of King Arthur and his knights. Their picture was fostered by the poetic works of people like Alfred, Lord Tennyson and the paintings of the Pre-Raphaelites. Their image in turn was based upon that of earlier writers and artists. Yet the image that they portray is quite distinctly that of knights in shining armour, albeit the armour of the Fourteenth and Fifteenth Centuries rather than of the so-called Dark Ages of the Sixth Century in which we are led to believe that Arthur thrived.

So let us have a look at those earlier writers and the writers who followed them all the way up to today, because they do not all tell the same tale. Different writers seem to introduce different elements and different characters.

Lost in translation?

It is worth noting that the many sources that have formed the pool of work from which the Arthurian tales have been drawn have been written in different languages. This perhaps makes some distortion likely, since it allows for different interpretations as works are translated from one language to another.

We will make a note on the language in which the source was written.

Historical chronicles or romance?

Before we delve into the early literature we have to ask what sort of material we are looking at. Works like Lord Tennyson's *Idylls of the King* and Sir Thomas Malory's *Le Morte d'Arthur* are clearly pieces of fiction. Tennyson's is an epic poem and Malory's is one of the first recognisable novels in English. It is unlikely if either of these authors saw their work as an historical record. More likely they considered their work to be retellings of the Arthurian stories.

Yet the sources that they used were far older and far harder to categorise as fiction. Some of the sources were unashamed pieces of literature based on ballads and earlier romances. Others were clearly written as historical records. This is where the difficulty lies, for mentions here and there in ancient documents about Arthur, various battles and various places make it seem as if there could be truth in some of the story that has come down to us.

This is an important point, since the name of King Arthur is so well known, the stories having been promulgated around the world. At one time it was taken for granted that he had been an actual king. It is simply that when historians started to go back to original documents, there really was scant evidence for his existence which, for a king of such importance, was strange to say the least.

An ancient Welsh poem (*written in Old and Middle Welsh*)

The first mention of Arthur – note that this is just Arthur, not King Arthur – is found in a single stanza of a poem that is called *Y Gododdin*. A single manuscript exists which is called *The Book of Aneirin*. Aneirin is thought to have been the poet who wrote it.

It recounts a battle fought in about the year 600 AD, near to Catterick in the north of England, between the Gododdin, a tribe of warriors from the south of Scotland and the Angles. He refers to the battle as Catraeth. The famed stanza written in medieval Welsh reads thus:

> *He fed black ravens on the ramparts of a fortress*
> *Though he was no Arthur*
> *Among the powerful ones*
> *In the front rank, Gwarddur was a palisade.*

The poem means that the hero Gwarddur fought and killed many, feeding their carcases to the ravens on the battlefield, yet he was not the equal of Arthur. The battle was a disaster for the Gododdin who had attacked the Angle stronghold. They were almost wiped out.

The reference to Arthur implies that he was already regarded as a mighty warrior before the year 600. This is a tantalising snippet of information because, although it is a poem not a chronicle, it implies that all should have heard of this previous mighty warrior.

The Battle of Catraeth

The significance of the battle of Catraeth is that it was one of the last battles fought by the Britons against the Saxons.

This battle has been used as a focal point by several modern novelists.

- John James – *Men of Cattreth*, 1969
- Rosemary Sutcliffe – *The Shining Company*, 1990
- Richard J Denning – *The Amber Treasure*, 2010

Gildas the Wise *(written in Latin)*

The next snippet of information is actually a piece of non-information.

Gildas was a cleric who wrote about post-Roman Britain in his book *De Excidio et Conquestu Britanniae* in the mid-Sixth Century. He mentions a war leader called Ambrosius Aurelianus who fought against the Saxons. He also writes about the great Battle of Mons Badonicus, which later commentators identified with Arthur.

Gildas makes no mention of Arthur which is odd, since he would have been contemporary with him. Not to mention him would be unforgiveable – unless he did not exist.

The Anglo-Saxons

Many people brought up on a diet of films about Robin Hood would consider that the true English race were the Anglo-Saxons, since Robin Hood waged a sort of guerrilla war against the invading Normans, or at least against King John and his Norman barons when he tried to usurp the throne from King Richard in the early Thirteenth Century. Robin Hood has little to do with this book, apart from the fact that he too has achieved legendary status and has transcended any historical basis that he may have had.

The other point is that Britain has over the centuries been invaded many times. Arthur is considered to have been a leader of the native Britons. Yet the Britons were not obviously one people, but would have been an amalgam of indigenous people and Romans. When the Romans left Britain, some upper class Britons of Roman ancestry – such as Ambrosius Aurelianus, perhaps – could have waged war against the invaders who came after the Roman legions had been called home.

The Britons – and Arthur was supposedly King of the Britons – fought against these invaders, the Angles, Saxons and Jutes, defeating them at the great battle of Mons Battonicus in about 550 AD.

- The Angles came from Angeln, or modern Germany
- The Saxons came from Lower Saxony, or modern Germany and the Low Countries
- The Jutes from the Jutland peninsula, or modern Denmark

The Battle of Mount Badon

This was a very real battle although the exact date is not known. It took place sometime between 490 and 550 AD. It was the last major win by the Britons against the Saxons. It is referred to by historians as Mons Badonicus and by writers of the stories as Mount Badon. It may have been fought at Bath.

Gildas mentions it, as does the Venerable Bede, who wrote the *Ecclesiastical History of England*, but neither of them identifies the victor as Arthur. Nennius, however, does.

Eventually, the Britons' resistance was broken down sometime around 600 AD. After that the Anglo-Saxons ruled until 1066 when the Normans invaded England under William the Conqueror.

Nennius and his History of the Britons *(written in Latin)*

In about the year 800 AD Nennius wrote *Historia Brittonum*, or *The History of the Britons*. It is a very interesting piece of work. The translation by J.A. Giles, a Victorian scholar who also translated Bede's great work, gives a flavour of the author and his acknowledgement that there were other, greater scholars than he. In the prologue, he begins:

> *Nennius, the lowly minister and servant of the servants of God, by the grace of God, disciple of St Elbotus, to all the followers of truth sendeth health.*
> *Be it known to your charity, that being dull in intellect and rude of speech, I have presumed to deliver these things in the Latin tongue, not trusting to my own learning, which is little or none at all, but partly from traditions to our ancestors.*

Little of learning he may have said, yet his use of Latin indicated his considerable learning.

In his book he describes the ruler Vortigern, ruler of Powys, who invited the Saxons to help stave off attacks from the marauding Picts and northern tribes. He tells of how Horsa and Hengist arrived on the island of Thanet.

144

He names Arthur and twelve great battles that he fought, culminating in Mount Badon.

Then it was, that magnanimous Arthur, with all the kings and military force of Britain, fought against the Saxons. And though there were many more noble than himself, yet he was twelve times chosen their commander, and it was as often conqueror.

Is this the description of a king or of a general or generalissimo? Someone so skilled in battle and in leadership that even kings might follow him? It is possible. If that is the case it is a possible reason why his name would be missing from a chronicle of the kings. He may not have been one, but perhaps others thought that he should have been.

At any rate, Nennius tells that he is a mighty warrior. In describing the twelfth battle:

The twelfth was a most severe contest, when Arthur penetrated to the hill of Badon. In this engagement, nine hundred and forty fell by his hand alone, no one but the Lord affording him assistance. In all these engagements the Britons were successful. For no strength can avail against the will of the Almighty.

Note the importance that Nennius ascribes to the right of might that is given to the true followers of Christianity.

The Mabinogion (written in Welsh)

This is a wonderful collection of eleven prose stories collected from medieval Welsh literature. They are of pre-Christian origin and give a superb insight into the pagan and Celtic roots of the people. Believed to have been written sometime between the mid-Eleventh and mid-Thirteenth Centuries, they are almost certainly written versions of much older tales that had been kept alive by the story-tellers and bards of Wales. They contain history, myth and legend told with the poetic beauty of the Welsh.

The word *'Mabinogion'* was coined by Lady Charlotte Guest (1812-1995) who translated the stories in the mid-Nineteenth Century. It is the plural of *'mabinogi'*, which means a story for the children.

There are two medieval manuscripts from which *The Mabinogion* as a collection has been garnered. One is called *The White Book of Rhydderch*, which has been dated to about 1325 and the other is *The Red Book of Hergest*, written in about 1380.

Within The *Mabinogion*, there are four interlinked tales referred to as *The Four Branches of the Mabinogi*. These tell of several famed Welsh royal heroes. Also within The *Mabinogion*, there are two other tales that concern Arthur.

Culhwch and Olwen

This is thought to have originated in the Eleventh Century, possibly making it one of the very earliest Arthurian tales. It concerns Prince Culhwch, a cousin of King Arthur who seeks out his help to find the beautiful Olwen with whom he is in love although he has never seen her. Within the tale two hundred of King Arthur's knights are named. Arthur sends six knights to help his cousin. These include:

* Cai – identified as Sir Kay
* Bedwyr – identified as Sir Bedivere
* Gwalchmei – identified as Sir Gawain

The Dream of Rhonabwy

This tale was written in the Twelfth or Thirteenth Centuries and is set during the reign of Madog, the Prince of Powys in the mid-Twelfth Century. Rhonabwy is a servant of Madog who is sent to find the Prince's rebellious brother. One night he has a dream when he is transported back to the days of Arthur, almost to the eve of the Battle of Mount Badon. King Arthur is playing chess with Owain, whom we can identify as Sir Uwain. The tale has a dream quality to it that makes interpretation difficult. Yet its significance to us is that it again refers back to an historical event and places Arthur at its heart.

The Black Book of Carmarthen (written in Welsh)

This was a compilation of poems written in Welsh in the Thirteenth Century. There are mentions of adventures of Arthur and also, in

The Stanza of the Graves, there is mention of the graves of Gwalchmai (Gawain), of Owain, son of Urien, of Bedwyr (Bedivere) and of Arthur. It specifically mentions that Arthur's is a wonder. The actual word used is *'anoeth'*, which could be interpreted as meaning it is difficult to find. If the latter is the case then it could imply that Arthur is not dead, merely sleeping in a mystical state. This could be the origin of the belief that King Arthur and his knights are merely slumbering, waiting for the day when they will be needed again.

The Book of Taliesin (written in Welsh)

This is another famous Welsh text from the Fourteenth Century, apparently based on the works of the Sixth Century poet, Taliesin.

Now Taliesin has been called King Arthur's bard, since he would have been contemporary with the king. There are some references to Arthur in one of the poems called *The Spoils of Annwn*. In it Arthur has to travel to Annwn, 'the Fort of Glass' to retrieve a magical cauldron and sword.

The Annals of Wales (written in Latin)

The Annales Cambriae or *The Annals of Wales* are a set of chronicles written in Latin in about 970 AD. The manuscript is kept in the British Museum. It details events that occurred in Wales, Ireland, Scotland and England between the years 447-954 AD.

It has three fascinating entries, two mentioning Arthur, one also mentioning Mordred, and one about Merlin.

- For the year 516 – The Battle of Badon, in which Arthur carried the Cross of our Lord Jesus Christ for three days and three nights on his shoulders and the Britons were the victors
- For the year 537 – The Battle of Camlann, in which Arthur and Medraut fell; and there was plague in Britain and Ireland
- For the year 573 – The Battle of Arfderydd between the sons of Eliffer and Gwenddolau son of Ceidio; in which battle Gwenddolau fell; Merlin went mad

For many years these were regarded as being historically accurate but scholars have serious doubts about the document which contains much obscure information. It is still regarded by many people as proof not only of Arthur's existence but also of key elements in the Arthurian saga.

Geoffrey of Monmouth *(written in Latin)*

In about 1135 the Welsh cleric Geoffrey of Monmouth wrote *Historia Regum Britanniae*, or *The History of the Kings of Britain*. He revised it over the following dozen years so that it was completed in 1147. It was to be the most significant source for Arthur for several hundred years and since it contained a fairly detailed account of Arthur and his reign, alongside that of other known kings, it was accepted as being the true history of the kings of Britain.

Geoffrey refers to himself as *'Galfridus Monumentensis'* which means Geoffrey of Monmouth. It is not known why he associates himself with the place, but it may be that was where he was born. In 1152 he was consecrated as Bishop of St Asaph.

Certainly Geoffrey was a scholar of note. In his book *The History of the Kings of Britain* he asserts that his writings were based upon 'an ancient book in the British language that told in orderly fashion the deeds of all the kings of Britain.' He claimed that this book had been given to him by Walter, Archdeacon of Oxford.

What the title of that book was or even whether it existed is unknown. Some modern scholars aver that it is fictitious and that much of what Geoffrey recounts is simply the product of his own fertile imagination. Yet that is perhaps being unfair to Geoffrey, for it may well have been an older work of romance that he may not have wished to refer to by name. He would, in addition, almost certainly have had access to the work of Gildas, Nennius and the Venerable Bede.

The book is nowadays thought by many Arthurian scholars to be a fanciful history, recounting:

- The settlement of Britain by Brutus, a descendent of the Trojan hero Aenas
- The tale of King Lear and his three daughters which was later told by William Shakespeare in his play, *King Lear*

- The tale of King Cymbeline, another King immortalised in a play by William Shakespeare
- The reign of Belinus who conquered Gaul from the Romans
- The reigns of King Constantine and of his three sons, Constans, Aurelius Ambrosius and Uther Pendragon
- The role of Vortigern
- The tale of Merlin
- The tale of King Arthur
- The reign and death of King Cadwalader

Geoffrey devotes about a third of the book to Arthur and establishes him as being conceived by Uther Pendragon, being born in Tintagel Castle in Cornwall and having a great court, a loyal band of knights, and a mystical adviser in Merlin. He recounts many tales of adventure, culminating in his mortal wound at the battle of Camlann, from where he is transported to the Isle of Avalon.

It has to be emphasised that Geoffrey may have had a reason for spending so much time on King Arthur and for recounting about Tintagel and its associations with King Arthur. His patron was Robert, Earl of Gloucester whose brother was Reginald, Earl of Cornwall. He could well have been establishing a pedigree for the new Norman aristocracy by linking them to the former rulers and the great King Arthur.

The Jersey-born poet Wace and the Round Table *(written in French)*

The poet Wace was born on the island of Jersey and lived in Normandy, eventually becoming the Canon of Bayeux. He wrote several works in French verse, including *Roman de Rou*, a history of the Dukes of Normandy and, in 1155, his great work *Roman de Brut*, a retelling of Geoffrey of Momouth's tales of King Arthur.

Significantly, he introduced two very important elements to the story:

- The Round Table
- The sword Excalibur

Chrétien de Troyes *(written in French)*

We do not know a lot about this French poet which is a great shame, for rather like the English poet Geoffrey Chaucer, he has a claim to be one of the first novelists. He flourished in the Twelfth Century and clearly had a significant knowledge, probably through personal experience, of courtly behaviour and life. It is thought that he served at the court of the Countess of Champagne between 1160 and 1172.

It was during and after this period that he became active as a poet. He wrote five major narrative poems in octosyllabic rhyming couplets between 1170 and 1181, when it is thought that he died.

These were:

- Erec et Enide – a tale of courtly love set in the court of King Arthur
- Cligès – a young knight falls in love with his uncle's wife
- Yvain – the Knight of the Lion
- Lancelot – the love affair between Lancelot and Guinevere at the court of King Arthur in Camelot
- Percival – the tale of the Grail; this was an unfinished work and the Grail is mentioned as a sort of salver

The poet Wace had introduced courtly love into the tales, yet Chrétien de Troyes developed this and introduced the idea of chivalry, holding it as an aspiration of knighthood.

He was also the first to talk about Camelot and to introduce the character of Lancelot and the love triangle that was to become such a part of the Arthurian tale.

William of Malmesbury *(written in Latin)*

We know more about this scholar and historian than we do about most of the early writers. He was born in about 1096 and died in about 1145. A monk at Malmesbury Abbey in Wiltshire, he is regarded as the finest historian of his day. Scholars have deduced that he based his writings on those of at least four hundred others, so there is little doubt that he approached history in the same way as do modern historians.

In the light of his academic credentials it is interesting that he describes Arthur and his role in the fight against the Saxons, naming the battle of Mount Badon. He also describes the grave of Gawain upon a shore.

Robert de Boron and the Holy Grail *(written in French verse)*

It was another poet who would develop the idea of the Holy Grail as the cup of Christ. The Burgundian poet Robert de Boron thrived in the late Twelfth Century. Rather like Chrétien de Troyes, we do not know a great deal about him except that he wrote poetry, was probably born in the town of Boron, and that he went with his master to fight in the Fourth Crusade where he probably met his death.

There are two surviving poems:

- Joseph of Arimathea – who brought the Holy Grail to England
- Merlin – about the great magician, although only a few fragments survive

He wrote about the Holy Grail, stating that it was the cup that was used by Christ at The Last Supper.

There is a verse fragment mentioning Percival and so it can be seen how the tale of The Holy Grail was developed.

He also introduced the idea of the sword in the stone, although he actually has it stuck in an anvil atop the stone. In addition, he mentions the Siege Perilous, the seat which only the Grail Knight may sit upon.

It is thought that he had probably written or intended to write two other poems, one about Percival and one about the death of Arthur. He probably wrote enough to stimulate the creativity of other authors.

Layamon and the glory of battle (written in English)

In the late Twelfth Century, an English priest named Layamon wrote a long alliterative poem entitled *Brut*, presumably after Chrétien de Troyes' *Le Roman de Brut*. In it he revels in the glory of battles and warfare. His style is at times quite gruesome. He also mentions the Round Table which he claimed could hold 1,600 Knights, and that Arthur's court was based in London.

Most significantly, he was the first person to write in English, thereby potentially making the story more available, albeit in times when literacy and access to literature was very low.

Merlin dictating his prophesies to his scribe, Blaise; Thirteenth Century miniature from Robert de Boron's *Merlin en Prose.*

The Vulgate Cycle *(written in French)*

Between the years 1215 and 1235, a group of anonymous Cistercian monks wrote a series of five Arthurian romances. These seem to have been based on the works of Geoffrey of Monmouth, Robert de Boron and Wace.

- *The History of the Holy Grail*
- *The Story of Merlin*
- *Lancelot (and other Knights of the Round Table)*
- *The Quest for the Holy Grail*
- *The Death of Arthur*

The story that they produce, since the five volumes are interwoven, gives us a very clear sense of good and evil in the adulterous acts of Lancelot and Guinevere and of Tristram and Isolde, and the duplicity of Mordred, as compared with the virtuous lives led by Percival and Galahad. The Holy Grail is symbolic of the quest for Christian goodness and the whole saga hinges on the ideals of chivalry, good deeds and fellowship. The Grail and the Round Table are linked and the part that Merlin plays in the whole saga is clear. He manufactures the Round Table, complete with the special Sieges for each knight, and especially the Siege Perilous that only the Grail Knight may sit upon.

King Arthur takes a lesser role in these romances, whereas many of the other knights are introduced as they go about their various quests. However, the love triangle between Lancelot and Guinevere and King Arthur is of paramount importance, as is the falling apart of the Round Table, the ultimate destruction of Camelot and the death of Arthur.

King Arthur and the Round Table – products of the Medieval Age

We very much have an image of King Arthur and his Knights of the Round Table as people who lived in the medieval period. Historians are not actually in agreement as to how to categorise the different times. Although Arthur seems to have flourished in the Sixth Century, yet most of his depictions seem to be from a time somewhere between the Twelfth and Fifteenth Centuries. That is understandable, since that is the time when the tales seem to have been drawn together like a great patchwork quilt, and embellished and set down as a sort of history.

There is something more that one needs to consider, of course, and that is why the tales developed as they did. It is very much to do with the structure of society at the time.

The Norman Conquest of 1066 marked a colossal change in British society. England was invaded and conquered and the new ruling elite carved up the country into a series of large estates. The country was systematically catalogued and an audit taken of the wealth of every hamlet, village and town the length of the land in the *Domesday Book*.

The noted historian Charles Homer Hasking discussed the importance of this time in his 1928 book, *The Renaissance of the Twelfth Century*. It is regarded as a landmark book in history. Essentially, starting in the mid-Eleventh Century, this is described as the Central or High Middle Ages.

A very definite structure was then imposed upon society, consisting of three elements:

- The knighthood or *chevalerie*
- The Church or *clergie*
- The people who laboured

This three-layered society was what the Norman overlords imposed and needed to work. Note the word *'chevalerie'*, for this is the essence of knighthood at the time. It was that strata of society that ruled and policed the system. They were all powerful. From this we get the beginnings of chivalry. The Norman lords began a system of castle building. They erected motte and bailey castles all over England which were easily built, economical and effective.

Next we have *'clergie'*, meaning the Church. This was the Norman Church and it was important to establish its credentials. Accordingly Norman Churches were built all over the country, in all of the new towns. It was important to establish authority over the people who laboured and one of the most effective ways was through creating an ordered religion that would link up with the *chevalerie*. Hence *clergie* and *chevalerie* went hand in hand.

And so here we have the importance of King Arthur and the way in which the tales were told. The French romances were amalgamated with the Welsh and Celtic tales, and the Christian message was firmly threaded through them. The new Norman aristocracy also needed to establish their pedigree by showing the links that they had with the people who were there before the Saxons. This meant the world of King Arthur. In the tales the links with Troy and later with France were established with Arthur and his knights. Naturally, the Norman knights were seen as merely returning to the land of their earlier counterparts.

And in the Tales of King Arthur there was an inevitable intermingling of values of *chevalerie* and *clergie*, which developed into the ideas of chivalry and piety – which became the cornerstones of knighthood.

Who better to get to write these tales than clerics or priests who enjoyed the patronage of the knights? Geoffrey of Monmouth, for example, enjoyed the patronage of Robert, Earl of Gloucester, the brother of Gerald, first Earl of Cornwall, who owned Tintagel Castle.

And thus King Arthur being born in Tintagel formed the link and helped to give the people who laboured a reason for venerating both the high order of chivalry and the beneficence of the Church.

England was ready to claim King Arthur as its hero and greatest ever king. You will see that these ideals must have been very much in the psyche of the next great writer who took up the cause of King Arthur, Sir Thomas Malory.

From the melee to the joust

Jousting seems to have been very much a way of life in the Arthurian saga. Knights tilted lances at each other, both in organised tournaments or out in the open countryside, in the shadows of castles, in leafy glades and beside rivers. It is doubtful that such chivalrous fighting would have been commonplace in Fifth Century Arthurian Britain.

The Melee, Eglinton Tournament, by James Henry Nixon, 1839.

Jousting is actually a martial game or exercise between two mounted knights bearing long lances. It had its beginnings in the Eleventh Century, in the East, when such combats were arranged on camels. It was only later in the Twelfth Century that horse-mounted knights followed suit.

The melee was the name given to a mass combat, a sort of free-for all lacking organisation or tactics, which preceded the development of the joust. Its aim was for individual knights to capture other knights and hold them for ransom. Not in a 'dungeons and imprisonment' style of ransom, more in the manner of a game, where removal of a knight from the field would result in him being honour bound to pay a ransom.

Sir William Marshal (1147–1219), first Earl of Pembroke, was a master of the melee and a champion knight. Stephen Langton, the Archbishop of Canterbury at the time, called him the 'greatest knight that ever lived.' He served four kings of England and became Regent of England for King Henry III. He is featured in the 2010 film Robin Hood, starring Russell Crow as the famed outlaw and William Hurt as William Marshal.

Jousting became organised into a real sport in the Late Middle Ages and tournaments were held until the Seventeenth Century. They were spectacular events staged by the nobility, even being used to celebrate the marriage of King Charles I.

In 1839 Archibald William Montgomerie, the Thirteenth Earl of Eglinton and Winton staged a glorious tournament at Eglinton Castle in Ayreshire, featuring medieval processions, a melee and jousting. Tens of thousands of spectactors came to watch.

Sir Thomas Malory and Le Morte d'Arthur

We come now to Sir Thomas Malory (c1405-1470), one of the most important writers in the whole of Arthurian literature, and his great work, *Le Morte d'Arthur*.

This masterful piece, which draws together many of the strands supplied by some of the other writers that we have looked at so far, is the version of the Arthurian saga with which most people are familiar. It was printed by William Caxton in 1485.

It is a huge book of some 300,000 words, written by Sir Thomas Malory mainly during times of imprisonment for various misdemeanors. Although it is now thought of as being a single work, most Arthurian scholars seem to consider that it was written by him as a collection of tales.

The puzzling titles

The book has had several titles, which may be puzzling.

- Its full title is, *The Birth, Life and Acts of King Arthur, of his noble knights of the Round Table, their marvellous Enquests and Adventures; th'Achieving of the Sangreal, and in the end the Dolorous Death and departing out of the World of them all*
- Caxton published it as *Le Morte Darthur*, without an apostrophe
- The Winchester Version edited by Eugène Vinaver was published as *Malory Works* in 1947
- The book is now generally known as *Le Morte d'Arthur*

William Caxton edited it into twenty-one separate books, which he subdivided into about 500 short chapters, each of which had an appealing chapter heading.

The strange case of the Winchester Manuscript

Caxton's printed version of the book and the subsequent reprinting by various publishers over the ensuing centuries maintained that format. Then in 1934, when the library at Winchester College was being recatalogued, the headmaster W. F. Oakeshott (later to become Sir William Fraser Oakeshott) discovered a manuscript of the great book. Oakeshott found that it was not divided into the twenty-one chapters as the Caxton versions had been, although he concluded that it seemed to have been previously divided into sections, possibly by Sir Thomas Malory himself.

Eugène Vinaver, a noted Arthurian scholar, then asked to examine the manuscript. He

The first page of William Caxton's printing of Malory's *Morte d'Arthur*, 1485.

157

came to a similar conclusion and was permitted to publish a version of the book, which he thought would be similar to the version that Malory had intended.

The clues they found in the continuous text of the Winchester Version were small 'explicits,' or explanatory paragraphs that had been inked in at the end of various sections. These seemed to have been written by Malory himself, and indicate points where he felt stories naturally ended. They also tended to refer to him.

There were eight of these explicits and each one of them is very interesting. They allowed Vinaver to divide 'the work' into eight 'books'. Caxton excluded them from his version but put in an amalgamated one, which gave no clue about how the work had originally been divided. He had clearly exerted editorial control over his author's work.

These books were as follows, with some of the explicits that give a clue about Malory's plight.

1) THE TALE OF KING ARTHUR

HERE ENDYTH THIS TALE, AS THE FREYNCHE BOOK SEYETH, FRO THE MARYAGE OF KYNGE UTHER UNTO KYNGE ARTHURE THAT REGNED AFTIR HYM AND DED MANY BATAYLES.

AND THIS BOOKE ENDYTH WHEREAS SIR LAUNCELOT AND SIR TRYSTRAMS COM TO COURTE. WHO THAT WOLL MAKE ONY MORE LETTEE HYM SEKE OTHER BOOKIS OF KYNGE ARTHURE OR OF SIR LAUNCELOT OR SIR TRYSTRAMS; OR THIS WAS DRAWYN BY A KNYGHT PRESONER, SIR THOMAS MALLEORÉ, THAT GOD SNDE HYM GOOD RECOVER. AMEN. EXPLICIT.

2) THE TALE OF THE NOBLE KING ARTHUR THAT WAS EMPEROR HIMSELF THROUGH DIGNITY OF HIS HANDS

3) THE NOBLE TALE OF SIR LANCELOT DU LAKE

4) THE TALE OF SIR GARETH OF ORKNEY THAT WAS CALLED BEWMAYNES

AND I PRAY YOU ALL THAT REDYTH THIS TALE TO PRAY FOR HYM THAT THIS WROTE, THAT GOD SENDE HYM GOOD DELYVERAUNCE SONE AND HASTELY. AMEN.
HERE ENDYTH THE TALE OF SIR GARETH OF ORKNEY.

5) THE BOOK OF SIR TRYSTRAM DE LYONES

HERE ENDYTH THE SECUNDE BOKE OFF SYR TRYSTRAM DE LYONES, WHYCHE DRAWYNE WAS OUTE OF FREYNSHE BY SIR THOMAS MALLEORÉ, KNYGHT, AS JESU BE HYS HELPE. AMEN.
BUT HERE YS NO REHERSALL OF THE THIRDE BOOKE.
BUT HERE FOLLOWYTH THE NOBLE TALE OFF THE SANKEGREALL, WHYCHE CALLED YS THE HOLY VESSELL AND THE SYGNYFUCACION OF BLESSED BLOODE OFF OURE LORDE JESU CRYSTE, WHYCHE WAS BROUGHT INTO THIS LONDE BY JOSEPH OF ARAMATHYE.
THEREFORE ON ALL SYNFULL, BLESSED LORDE, HAVE ON THY KNYGHT MERCY. AMEN.

6) THE TALE OF THE SANKGREAL BRIEFLY DRAWN OUT OF FRENCH WHICH IS A TALE CHRONICLED FOR ONE OF THE TRUEST AND ONE OF THE HOLIEST THAT IS IN THIS WORLD

7) THE BOOK OF SIR LANCELOT AND QUEEN GUINEVERE

AND HERE ON THE OTHIR SYDE FOLOWYTH THE MOSTE PYTEUOUS TALE OF THE MORTE ARTHURE SAUNZ GWERDON PAR LE SHYVALERE SIR THOMAS MALLEORÉ, KNYGHT.
JESU, AYEDE LY PUR VOPUTRE BONE MERCY! AMEN.

8) THE MOST PITEOUS TALE OF THE MORTE ARTHURE SAUNZ GWERDON

HERE IS THE ENDE OF THE HOOLE BOOK OF KYNG ARTHURE AND HIS NOBLE KNYGHTES OF THE ROUNDE TABLE, THAT WHAN THEY WERE HOLE TOGYDERS THERE WAS EVER AN HONDRED AND FORTY. AND HERE IS THE ENDE OF THE DETH OF ARTHURE.
I PRAYE YOU ALL JENTYLMEN AND JENTTYLWYMMEN THAT REDETH THIS BOOK OF ARTHURE AND HIS KNYGHTES FROM THE BEGYNNYNG TO THE ENDYNGE, PRAYE FOR ME WHYLE I AM ON LYVE THAT GOD SENDE ME GOOD DELYVERAUNCE AND WHAN I AM DEED, I PRAYE YOU ALL PRAYE FOR MY SOULE.
FOR THIS BOOK WAS ENDED THE NINTH YERE OF THE REYGNE OF KING EDWARD THE FOURTH, BY SIR THOMAS MALLEORÉ, KNYGHT, AS JESU HELPE HYM FOR HYS GRETE MYGHT, AS HE IS THE SERVAUNT OF JESU BOTHE DAY AND NYGHT.

The Joust between the Lord of the Tournament and the Knight of the Red Rose.

Although he writes that the book is set 454 years after the passion of Christ (that period of Christ's suffering between the Garden of Gethsemane and the Crucifixion), Malory describes the characters as acting, living and dressing much as would the gentlefolk of his own time. The book is his idea of how life should be led. He draws from 'the French book', presumably the works of Chrétien de Troyes, and uses the ideals of courtly love, honour and behaviour that were enunciated there as being the ideals of knighthood.

He writes about the great institution of the Round Table, and of Camelot as being how it should be, yet as a mere mortal he realises that few men can aspire to be truly great and worthy. Even the mighty Sir Lancelot has a weakness. He and Queen Guinevere transgress and they sow the seeds of destruction.

Yet in *The Quest for The Holy Grail*, the ultimate aim for The Round Table, he shows how men should aspire and try to be as good as possible, for only then can true peace and nobility be obtained. The importance of religion cannot be overestimated in the book, which is perfectly understandable considering the times in which that he wrote it. The Church was one of the great powerhouses of society and no-one would have doubted the existence of the Holy Grail or of its miraculous ability to heal.

Sir Thomas Malory's great work is the blueprint that has been used by Arthurian writers since the late Fifteenth Century.

Will the real Sir Thomas Malory please stand up?

Surprisingly little is known about the author of this great work, *Le Morte d'Arthur*. We have no contemporary portrait, no personal artefacts and no relics. We are actually not entirely sure which Thomas Malory he was, since we do know that there were at least six men called Thomas Malory living in the Fifteenth Century. As we have seen in the explicits above, the author of Le Morte d'Arthur was not always consistent in the spelling of his name. Only one of that name, however, was a knight, and that is a crucial point.

The search for the real Malory has incited a lot of speculation over the years. In the Sixteenth Century, the antiquarian and biographer John Leland suggested that Malory was Welsh. In 1984, an American scholar, G. T. Kitteridge suggested that he was in fact English and that he was Sir Thomas Malory of Newbold Revel, a manor near Coventry in the county of Warwickshire.

It was a highly respectable pedigree for an author of such a landmark book in English literature. Various facts could be ascertained from this that made him seem a reasonably wholesome individual. For example, he was known to have fought at Calais in 1414 (although he would have been a youngster of perhaps ten tears); he was a Member of Parliament for Warwickshire in 1445 and he died on the 14th March 1470 and was interred at Greyfriars Church in Newgate, London. His tombstone read:

Here lies a valiant knight

HIC JACET DOMINUS THOMAS MALLERE, VALENS MILES
OB 14 MAR 1470 DE PAROCHIA DE MONKENKIRBY IN COM
WARICINI

[Here lies Sir Thomas Mallere, Valiant Knight. Died 14 March 1470, in the parish of Monkenkirby in the county of Warwick]

Then in 1924 Edward Hicks, another American scholar, turned up some evidence that suggested that Malory had an altogether seedier if not downright sinister side to his personality. He discovered a degraded document in the Public Record's Office in London which listed a whole catalogue of crimes committed by Sir Thomas Malory. These included:

- being involved in a gang that had intended to ambush and murder the Duke of Buckingham
- breaking into the Abbey of Blessed Mary of Coombe where he stole valuables from the abbot's chest

161

- that he raped the wife of Hugh Smith
- that he frequently led cattle raids and was an extortionist

He was imprisoned on no fewer than eight occasions, with sentences ranging from a few days to two and a half years.

It is also recorded that he was a man of martial prowess, for he broke out of prison on two occasions. Once, on 27th July 1451 he escaped and swam across the moat at Coleshill prison. On another occasion, in October 1454, he broke out of Colchester by using great skill with a variety of weapons, including sword, daggers and langues-de-boeuf, a type of halberd with a spiked head the shape of an ox-tongue.

He was again imprisoned in 1460, the same year that Richard, Duke of York was killed at the Battle of Wakefield. This happened to be one of the main battles at the start of the Wars of the Roses, in which the Houses of Lancaster and York fought for the throne of England. In 1462 he fought with the Earl of Warwick, known to history as 'the king-maker,' on the side of the Yorkists. Soon after, Warwick changed allegiance to fight for the Lancastrians under Henry VI and Margaret of Anjou against King Edward IV. In 1468 and again in 1470 King Edward issued general pardons to Lancastrian rebels, but on both occasions Sir Thomas Malory was excluded by name. He was not one to have profited from the Wars of the Roses, for he died during the years of Yorkist supremacy.

It is thought highly likely that it was during some of his imprisonments that he started writing his great work. Yet this unsavoury reputation must have raised questions as well as eyebrows. Although there have been many writers with a criminal history, the suggestion that Malory could have been a rapist did not sit well with his image as a writer. An author who had been imprisoned for his beliefs or for just happening to be on the wrong side was one thing, but an abuser of women was quite another. So began the search for alternate Malory contenders.

We need not get bogged down in this debate. Professor Peter Field published his 1993 book *The Life and Times of Sir Thomas Malory*, in which he seems to prove that Sir Thomas Malory of Newbold Revel is the author.

So what of his besmirched reputation? Well, it may be that that is exactly what it was, a deliberate smearing campaign such as happened in times of war. The Wars of the Roses was a particularly brutal time when the victors took the spoils and the vanquished lost everything, often even their lives.

The Tudors who gained the throne when King Richard III was defeated and killed at Bosworth Field in 1485 wrote the history that they wanted to have recorded for later generations. First Thomas More with his book *The History of King Richard the Third* and then William Shakespeare with his play *The Tragedy of King Richard III* effectively created the image of the defeated Yorkist king as the most evil uncle in history, by suggesting that he had ordered the murder of his nephews, the Princes in the Tower. The veracity of the tale is hotly debated even today.

The point is that lesser beings than kings may have kept their lives, yet been castigated in other ways for their allegiance to the other side. Sir Thomas Malory's list of misdemeanors is long and his imprisonments may or may not have been deserved. Academics say that the crime of rape had a very different meaning in the Fifteenth Century and he may not have been the depraved criminal that is suggested in the list of his crimes. He may have been no worse than many another knight of his day. Indeed, perhaps his work *Le Morte d'Arthur* gives us a clue, in that Sir Lancelot, the knight with whom he seems to most closely identify himself, was a flawed character, just like most human beings.

Yet Malory was certainly a genius of a writer.

The play that Shakespeare never wrote

That towering genius of Elizabethan England, William Shakespeare, wrote plays about everything and everyone of importance. Histories, tragedies, comedies and stories from myths and legends, he wrote about them all. He wrote about early kings from Britain's Dark Ages. *King Lear* is based upon the mythical pre-Roman King Leir, and *Cymbeline* is based upon the life of the actual King Cunobelinus. Both are mentioned in Geoffrey of Monmouth's work *Historia Regum Britanniae*, or the *History of the Kings of Britain*. Why did he not write a play about King Arthur? It is a puzzle.

Yet there was one play with an Arthurian connection that was thought to have been written by William Shakespeare in collaboration with William Rowley. This was *The Birth of Merlin*, a Jacobean play first performed at the Curtain Theatre in Shoreditch, London in 1622. As the title implies, it concerns the birth of Merlin and it also includes Uther Pendragon,

Vortigern and Aurelius Ambrosius. It is occasionally performed, but no Shakespeare scholars accept it today as a Shakespeare play. Nonetheless, the Royal Shakespeare Company performed it at Stratford in 2010.

There is one possible reference to King Arthur in Henry V, Act II, scene iii, when news is received by Mistress Quickley about Sir John Falstaff's death.

Nay, sure, he's not in hell: he's in Arthur's bosom, if ever man went to Arthur's bosom.

[In 2011 Arthur Phillips wrote a novel entitled *The Tragedy of Arthur, King of Britain*. It is a quirky comic novel about a writer called Arthur Phillips (a fictionalised version of himself) who is asked to write the introduction to a newly discovered play by William Shakespeare.]

Edmund Spenser and *The Faerie Queen (written in English)*

The Tudor Age is a fascinating period in English history. King Henry VIII was intrigued by the Arthurian saga and the idea of jousting, chivalry and orders of knighthood. He even had himself depicted as Arthur on the Round Table that hangs in Winchester Great Hall.

Queen Elizabeth I supported the arts and oversaw a positive flowering of literary talent. William Shakespeare, Christopher Marlowe, Thomas Nashe and Ben Johnson were writing plays that would last for centuries. At the same time Edmund Spenser (1553-1599), a playboy poet, wrote *The Faerie Queen*, an allegorical poem about the Tudor dynasty in general and about Queen Elizabeth I in particular.

The Faerie Queen is a huge epic poem written in iambic pentameter. It is about chivalry, daring adventures, fabulous beasts, damsels in distress, knightly honour and courtly love. He published the first three books in 1590 and the second set of three books in 1596.

His intention was to write twelve books, each of which about one of King Arthur's knights who went on quests on behalf of the Faerie Queen, Gloriana. Gloriana was one of the names by which Queen Elizabeth I was known. Unfortunately, Edmund Spenser died in 1599 before he could finish his seventh book which he had started to plan in 1597.

Literary Sources

John Dryden, the librettist (written in English)

The next major writer was John Dryden (1631-1700), a poet, playwright and librettist of the Restoration Period. He was made Poet Laureate in 1667. His contribution to the Arthurian story was by writing the libretto to a semi-opera called *King Arthur, or The British Worthy.* The music was by Henry Purcell (1659-1695) and it was first performed at the Queen's Theatre, Dorset Garden, London in 1691.

The opera is not based upon the tales recounted by Malory but upon Arthur as King of the Britons in his battle against the Saxons. Merlin is a character, as are both Cupid and Venus.

Its significance is twofold. Firstly, by being the subject of an opera it brought Arthur to a wider audience. Secondly, since it is widely thought to be an allegorical tale relating to political events around the time of the Restoration of the monarchy after the English Civil Wars, it illustrates, in the same way as Spenser's *Faerie Queen* does, the way in which Arthur was used as a means for an author to deliver his own message. It shows how well established King Arthur was in the national psyche.

Alfred Lord Tennyson and *Idylls of the King (written in English blank verse)*

It was another Poet Laureate who really put life into King Arthur and the Knights of the Round Table when he wrote a series of twelve narrative poems about them between 1856 and 1885. They are collectively known as *Idylls of the King.* He dedicated the work to the late Prince Albert, the Crown Consort.

- *The Coming of Arthur*
- *Gareth and Lynette*
- *The Marriage of Geraint*
- *Geraint and Enid*
- *Balin and Balen*
- *Merlin and Viviene*
- *Lancelot and Elaine*
- *The Holy Grail*
- *Pelleas and Ettare*
- *The Last Tournament*

- *Guinevere*
- *The Passing of Arthur*

Tennyson based his work on Malory and *The Mabinogian*. He adapted it to his own purpose, however, telling the tales the way that he thought they should be told.

His interest in King Arthur seems to have been life-long. He also wrote shorter stand-alone poems such as *Sir Lancelot and Queen Guinevere* in 1830, *The Lady of Shalott* in 1833, *Sir Galahad* in 1842 and *Merlin and the Gleam* in 1889. Indeed, it seems that *Idylls of the King* had several starting points, including the shorter poem *Le Morte d'Arthur* which he started writing in 1833 and published in 1842. It would become the second part of *The Passing of Arthur* in the later full version of *Idylls of the King*.

Tennyson altered the spelling of several of the characters to make them sound more in keeping with Victorian taste. He also changed some of the tales, including the ending in *Guinevere*; he has her escape to a convent and later pardoned by Arthur, whereas Malory has her sentenced to the stake and rescued by Lancelot.

Idylls of the King is often regarded as being sombre in mood, which is in keeping with the nature of the poet and the Victorian age. As we saw earlier, Malory

Statue of Alfred, Lord Tennyson outside Lincoln Cathedral.

166

was an action man, a knight who had seen action and who reveled in the ideals of chivalry. Yet it was a different sort of chivalry from that envisaged and told by Tennyson.

Tennyson's poetry was complemented by the Pre-Raphaelite artists whose depictions of the Arthurian saga created an imagery that once again suited the Victorian concept of the age of Arthur.

Alfred, Lord Tennyson

To many people Alfred, Lord Tennyson (1809-1892) is the epitome of the Victorian poet. With his receding hair, almost Shakespearean brow, flowing locks and great beard he is immediately recognisable. He became Poet Laureate upon the death of William Wordsworth in 1850 and held the post until his death in 1892, at the age of eighty-three.

The fourth of twelve children, Alfred Tennyson was born on the 6th of August, 1809 at Sowerby in Lincolnshire. His father, the Reverend George Tennyson, was a Church of England rector; he was a man of many talents but he also had problems with excessive drinking and poorly controlled epilepsy. One of Alfred's brothers suffered a nervous breakdown and had to be committed to a mental asylum, and he himself was under the care of his doctor for some time in 1843 because of black moods. For this reason Alfred was ever fearful that 'madness' lurked within his family, or in the 'black blood' of the Tennysons. It would lead him to delay his own marriage.

Although the family lived well as a professional household, there was bitterness because the Reverend Tennyson had been disinherited by his father, Alfred's grandfather, in favour of his younger brother Charles. Thus, Alfred grew up feeling impoverished when compared with the wealth of his uncle. It is said that this made Alfred worry about money for the rest of his life, but especially so in the early years before his poetic genius was discovered.

He was somewhat relieved to follow his two elder brothers to Trinity College, Cambridge where he joined a secret society called *The Apostles*. This was an undergraduate group that met to discuss philosophy. Among their number was another budding poet, Arthur Hallam, who was already being hailed as a poet of some brilliance. They became great friends and Arthur duly became engaged to Alfred's sister Emily. Sadly, Hallam died in 1833 at the young age of twenty-two. This devastated

Alfred who channeled his grief into some of his best poems, including *In Memoriam* and *Ulysses*.

In the late 1830s he was quite concerned about his mental health and consulted a Dr Matthew Allen. Dr Allen was something of an entrepreneur and he had an idea to use steam power to mass-produce wood carvings. Alfred invested much of his inheritance in the venture which unfortunately soon went bankrupt. As a result, Alfred called off his engagement to his long-term sweetheart because he had no money. Later, in 1850 after he became Poet Laureate and had secured a Civil List pension and was making money from his work, he and Emily Sellwood married. They had two children, Hallam and Lionel.

Both Queen Victoria and Prince Albert were admirers of Tennyson's work. In 1853, when he and his wife moved to the Isle of Wight, Prince Albert actually called upon him unannounced. *Idylls of the King* took Victorian society by storm, and Tennyson dedicated it to Prince Albert who died in 1861.

In 1855 he wrote his famous poem *The Charge of the Light Brigade*, after the disastrous but heroic cavalry charge at the Battle of Balaclava during the Crimean War.

Tennyson twice turned down knighthoods offered by the Prime Minister, Benjamin Disraeli. In 1883 another great Prime Minister, William Gladstone put him forward for a peerage, which he accepted. In 1884 Queen Victoria created him Baron Tennyson, of Aldworth in the County of Sussex and of Freshwater in the Isle of Wight. Thus, he became Alfred, Lord Tennyson, the Poet Laureate.

T.H. White and The Once and Future King (written in English)

This is a more modern retelling of the Arthurian saga, based upon Malory's *Le Morte d'Arthur*. It may actually have done a great deal to bring the tales of King Arthur and the Knights of the Round Table to a larger, global audience. This is because his first Arthurian novel, *The Sword in the Stone*, was made into a highly successful Walt Disney animated film and his major work, *The Once and Future King*, was used as the basis for the musical *Camelot*, which was also was later made into a film.

Literary Sources

White followed up *The Sword in the Stone* with three other novels which together have been published as the epic work, *The Once and Future King.* Thus:

- *The Sword in the Stone*, 1938
- *The Witch in the Wood* (originally published as *The Queen of Air and Darkness*), 1939
- *The Ill-Made Knight*, 1940
- *The Candle in the Wind*, 1958

The Once and Future King, containing all four revised books, was published in 1958.

The Once and Future King

The Sword in the Stone tells the story of a young boy called Wart, who is befriended by a magician named Merlyn.

The Witch in the Wood tells of Arthur's reign from being crowned king. He invents the Round Table and defeats King Lot and others who rise against him.

The Ill-Made Knight is set in Camelot and revolves around Sir Lancelot and his adventures, including the Quest for the Holy Grail, and takes in the suicide of Elaine and his relationship with Guinevere.

The Candle in the Wind seemed to be the last book in *The Once and Future King.* It takes us from the discovery of Lancelot and Guinevere's adultery by Mordred and Agravaine to the very eve of the battle (of Camlann) on Salisbury Plain.

T.H. White died in 1964 and it was assumed that his work on the Arthurian saga was finished. Then, among his papers which had been left to the University of Texas, a fifth novel was discovered. This was *The Book of Merlyn* which had been written in 1941 but was not published until 1971.

The Book of Merlyn is quite a strange book. It is set on the very eve of the last great battle. Malory gives us a picture of Arthur sleeping fitfully and dreaming of Sir Gawain and receiving a message. T.H. White also has Arthur dreaming but he meets Merlyn, who takes him on a journey to review his life and to give him his final lessons. There are some strange moments when Arthur is metamorphosed into an ant in a colony and a goose in a flock of geese. These are allegorical tales, used by White to look at the futility of war, for he was writing this during the Second World War.

T.H. White

Thomas Hanbury White was born in 1906 in Bombay (modern Mumbai) in India, where his father was a member of the Indian Civil Service. He was educated in England at Cheltenham College and later graduated with a first class honours degree in English from Queens' College, Cambridge. Between 1930 and 1936 he taught English at Stowe School. In that year he gave up teaching in order to devote himself to full time writing.

White was a man of many interests. He immersed himself in a study of the Middle Ages, Arthurian literature, and in all the arts, crafts and sports appertaining to those times. He fished, hunted and learned how to plough a field with a horse-drawn plough.

He eventually retired to Alderney in the Channel Isles, where he lived until his death in 1964. He actually died on board a ship in Athens, on his way home from an American lecture tour.

Roger Lancelyn Green and King Arthur and his Knights of the Round Table *(written in English)*

Roger Lancelyn Green was an academic and a successful children's writer who wrote many books about myths and legends, bringing to life many heroes from different parts of the world for children in the post-Second World War era. In 1953 he wrote *King Arthur and his Knights of the Round Table*. This was an amalgamation of Malory, Welsh tales and medieval legends about King Arthur.

It was beautifully illustrated in medieval style by Lotte Reiniger.

Statue of King Arthur by Albrecht Dürer, 1512, Hofkirsche, Innsbruck.

Literary Sources

Roger Lancelyn Green

A group of academics used to meet in the corner of *The Eagle and Child*, a public house in Oxford. They called themselves *The Inklings* and their purpose, apart from enjoying a drink in congenial company, was to discuss literature. Among this circle of writers were J.R.R. Tolkien, who would write *The Lord of the Rings*, C.S. Lewis, who would write *The Chronicles of Narnia* and *The Space Trilogy*, and Roger Lancelyn Green, who would write many children's books including his retelling of the adventures of Robin Hood and of King Arthur.

Arthurian Art

Throughout this book you will have seen numerous depictions of King Arthur, his knights and of various tales. This is not surprising, since it is a very romantic story that just cries out to be illustrated.

William Caxton's 1485 Malory exists in two manuscripts – one held at the John Rylands Library in Manchester and the other at the Pierpont Morgan library in New York.

Wynkyn de Worde published the first illustrated *Le Morte d'Arthur* in 1498, with woodcuts specially prepared by an unknown artist known as 'the Arthur Cutter'. In 1816 the first two volume edition was published, illustrated by Thomas Unwins.

Aubrey Beardsley illustrated a modernised version of Caxton's *Le Morte d'Arthur* by Malory in 1893. In 1910 Sir William Russell Flint illustrated a version with watercolours and Arthur Rackham illustrated an edition in 1917.

The Pre-Raphaelites in the Nineteenth Century captured the mood of the era and re-invented the Arthurian image. They created an often mournful, romantic scenery that was ideal for the poetry of Tennyson and his *Idylls of the King*.

They were known as the Pre-Raphaelites because they wanted to recreate the spirit of art that flourished before Raphael. The three founders of the movement were Dante Gabriel Rossetti, John Millais and William Hunt. They were joined by others to form a brotherhood of seven, which inspired the movement.

King Arthur in sculpture and glass

- The most famous sculpture of King Arthur is a life-size statue in the Hofkirche, Innsbruck, designed by Albrecht Dürer and cast by Peter Vischer the Elder in about 1520
- There is a carved archway on the north portal of Modena Cathedral in Italy, depicting an Arthurian scene; beside one of the figures is the inscription *'Artus de Bretania'*, meaning Arthur of Britain
- There are many stained glass depictions of characters from the Arthurian saga, including ones by William Morris, Dante Gabriel Rossetti and Ford Madox Brown (see Page 44, *King Arthur and Sir Lancelot*, by William Morris; Page 51, *The fight between Sir Tristram and Sir Marhaus*, by Dante Gabriel Rossetti; and Page 52, *Sir Tristram and la Belle Ysoude*)

Roger Lancelyn Green was born in 1918 and studied under C.S. Lewis at Oxford. He came from an old English family and lived in a manor house in Cheshire that had belonged to the family for 900 years.

Chapter Eight
Arthurian Poetry

That story which the bold Sir Bedivere,
First made and latest left of all the knights,
Told, when the man was no more than a voice
In the white winter of his age, to those
With whom he dwelt, new faces, other minds.
        The Passing of Arthur, Idylls of the King,
                        Alfred, Lord Tennyson

IN THE last chapter we saw that some of the early sources for Arthur were poetic works. Now we shall look at some of the poems about King Arthur which have contributed to the oeuvre.

Sir Gawain and the Green Knight

The Pearl Poet (circa 1370-1400). Translated by Jessie L Weston (1850–1928)
We included the tale of Sir Gawain and the Green Knight in the first part of the book, although it was not included in Malory's Le *Morte d'Arthur* or Tennyson's *Idylls of the King.*

This is a Fourteenth Century poem which was written by an unknown poet, known in poetry and academic circles as either the 'Gawain poet', or the 'Pearl Poet'. This latter name comes from another poem called *Pearl*, which he wrote along with *Sir Gawain and the Green Knight, Patience* and *Cleanness.* They are written in alliterative verse, which means that alliteration is the main linkage between lines rather than rhyme.

The manuscript for *Sir Gawain and the Green Knight* is held in the British Library as *Cotton Nero A.x.* It is a small manuscript which is probably not the version written by the poet himself but by an unknown scribe. It is written in Middle English in a dialect that is placed somewhere in the middle of England, possibly even Cheshire. Although the tale is dealt with in Part One, it is worth looking at a couple of sections of the poem to get some flavour of the Middle English in which it was written.

The poem starts by talking about the siege of Troy, and tells how the noble Aeneas and his kin went adventuring, founding new civilizations including colonising Britain:

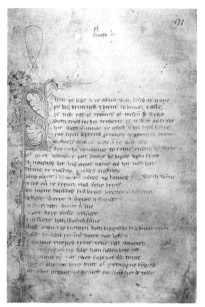

After the siege and the assault of Troy, when that burg was destroyed and burnt to ashes, and the traitor tried for his treason, the noble Aeneas and his kin sailed forth to become princes and patrons of well-nigh all the Western Isles. Thus Romulus built Rome (and

Sir Gawain and the Green Knight, first page from the *Cotton Nero A.x* manuscript, late Tenth Century.

gave to the city his own name, which it bears even to this day); and Ticius turned him to Tuscany; and Langobard raised him up dwellings in Lombardy; and Felix Brutus sailed far over the French flood, and founded the kingdom of Britain, wherein have been war and waste and wonder, and bliss and bale, ofttimes since.

And in that kingdom of Britain have been wrought more gallant deeds than in any other; but of all British kings Arthur was the most valiant, as I have heard tell, therefore will I set forth a wondrous adventure that fell out in his time. And if ye will listen to me, but for a little while, I will tell it even as it stands in story stiff and strong, fixed in the letter, as it hath long been known in the land.

The tale moves to the Court of King Arthur and the feasting of Christmas:

King Arthur lay at Camelot upon a Christmas-tide, with many a gallant lord and lovely lady, and all the noble brotherhood of the Round Table. There they held rich revels with gay talk and jest; one while they would ride forth

174

to joust and tourney, and again back to the court to make carols; for there was the feast holden fifteen days with all the mirth that men could devise, song and glee, glorious to hear, in the daytime, and dancing at night. Halls and chambers were crowded with noble guests, the bravest of knights and the loveliest of ladies, and Arthur himself was the comeliest king that ever held a court. For all this fair folk were in their youth, the fairest and most fortunate under heaven, and the king himself of such fame that it were hard now to name so valiant a hero.

Now the New Year had but newly come in, and on that day a double portion was served on the high table to all the noble guests, and thither came the king with all his knights, when the service in the chapel had been sung to an end. And they greeted each other for the New Year, and gave rich gifts, the one to the other (and they that received them were not wroth, that may ye well believe!), and the maidens laughed and made mirth till it was time to get them to meat. Then they washed and sat them down to the feast in fitting rank and order, and Guinevere the queen, gaily clad, sat on the high daïs. Silken was her seat, with a fair canopy over her head, of rich tapestries of Tars, embroidered, and studded with costly gems; fair she was to look upon, with her shining grey eyes, a fairer woman might no man boast himself of having seen.

And then comes the entrance of the fearsome Green Knight.

Now I will say no more of the service, but that ye may know there was no lack, for there drew near a venture that the folk might well have left their labour to gaze upon. As the sound of the music ceased, and the first course had been fitly served, there came in at the hall door one terrible to behold, of stature greater than any on earth; from neck to loin so strong and thickly made, and with limbs so long and so great that he seemed even as a giant. And yet he was but a man, only the mightiest that might mount a steed; broad of chest and shoulders and slender of waist, and all his features of like fashion; but men marvelled much at his colour, for he rode even as a knight, yet was green all over.

For he was clad all in green, with a straight coat, and a mantle above; all decked and lined with fur was the cloth and the hood that was thrown back from his locks and lay on his shoulders. Hose had he of the same green, and spurs of bright gold with silken fastenings richly worked; and all his vesture was verily green. Around his waist and his saddle were bands with fair stones set upon silken work, 'twere too long to tell of all the trifles that were embroidered thereon – birds and insects in gay gauds of green and gold. All the trappings of his steed were of metal of like enamel, even the stirrups that he stood in stained of the same, and stirrups and saddle-bow alike gleamed and shone with green stones. Even the steed on which he rode was of the same hue, a green horse, great and strong, and hard to hold, with broidered bridle, meet for the rider.

The knight was thus gaily dressed in green, his hair falling around his shoulders; on his breast hung a beard, as thick and green as a bush, and the beard and the hair of his head were clipped all round above his elbows. The lower part of his sleeves were fastened with clasps in the same wise as a king's mantle. The horse's mane was crisp and plaited with many a knot folded in with gold thread about the fair green, here a twist of the hair, here another of gold. The tail was twined in like manner, and both were bound about with a band of bright green set with many a precious stone; then they were tied aloft in a cunning knot, whereon rang many bells of burnished gold. Such a steed might no other ride, nor had such ever been looked upon in that hall ere that time; and all who saw that knight spake and said that a man might scarce abide his stroke.

The knight bore no helm nor hauberk, neither gorget nor breast-plate, neither shaft nor buckler to smite nor to shield, but in one hand he had a holly-bough, that is greenest when the groves are bare, and in his other an axe, huge and uncomely, a cruel weapon in fashion, if one would picture it. The head was an ell-yard long, the metal all of green steel and gold, the blade burnished bright, with a broad edge, as well shapen to shear as a sharp razor. The steel was set into a strong staff, all bound round with iron, even to the end, and engraved with green in cunning work. A lace was twined about it, that looped at the head, and all adown the handle it was clasped with tassels on buttons of bright green richly broidered.

The knight rideth through the entrance of the hall, driving straight to the high daïs, and greeted no man, but looked ever upwards; and the first words he spake were, 'Where is the ruler of this folk? I would gladly look upon that hero, and have speech with him.' He cast his eyes on the knights, and mustered them up and down, striving ever to see who of them was of most renown.

The poem reverberates with the themes of chivalry, seduction and honour. It gives an excellent account of medieval values.

There have been many writers who have translated and interpreted it, including J.R.R. Tolkien and E.V. Gordon, Norman Davis and, most recently, Simon Armitage in 2007.

The Lady of Shalott

Alfred, Lord Tennyson (1809-92)
Tennyson's *Idylls of the King* is an epic narrative poem. Before he wrote it he had written other shorter stand-alone poems, some of which he incorporated into *Idylls of the King.*

The *Lady of Shalott* is his earliest Arthurian poem. It is a ballad first written in twenty stanzas in 1833 and then rewritten with nineteen stanzas in 1842. It is based on Elaine of Astolat, who is the central character in *The Tale of Sir Lancelot and Elaine*, as recounted in Part One.

The poem is about a lady who lives in an enchanted castle on an island in the middle of a river that flows to Camelot. She has a curse upon her. She must knit a web and never look out of the castle on the world outside, other than through a mirror. One day she spies Sir Lancelot in the mirror and falls in love with him and actually looks out of the castle. The curse is then acted out and 'the mirror cracks from side to side.' Knowing that this means her death, she leaves the castle and gets into a barge where she writes her name, the Lady of Shalott. She lies down and dies and the barge floats down river, eventually coming to Camelot where all come out to see the mysterious, beautiful dead Lady of Shalott.

It is a brooding tale of unrequited love, for Sir Lancelot sees her and thinks that she has a lovely face, knowing nothing of her love for him. The poem may indeed tell us something about Tennyson and his own detached view of the world, which he depicts in the character of the Lady of Shalott who can only see the world through the reflection in the mirror.

Agatha Christie used the title *The Mirror Cracked* in one of her detective novels.

Part I

On either side the river lie
Long fields of barley and of rye,
That clothe the wold and meet the sky;
And thro' the field the road runs by
To many-tower'd Camelot;
And up and down the people go,
Gazing where the lilies blow
Round an island there below,
The island of Shalott.

Willows whiten, aspens quiver,
Little breezes dusk and shiver
Thro' the wave that runs for ever
By the island in the river
Flowing down to Camelot.
Four gray walls, and four gray towers,
Overlook a space of flowers,
And the silent isle imbowers
The Lady of Shalott.

By the margin, willow veil'd,
Slide the heavy barges trail'd
By slow horses; and unhail'd
The shallop flitteth silken-sail'd
Skimming down to Camelot:
But who hath seen her wave her hand?
Or at the casement seen her stand?
Or is she known in all the land,
The Lady of Shalott?

Only reapers, reaping early
In among the bearded barley,
Hear a song that echoes cheerly
From the river winding clearly,
Down to tower'd Camelot:
And by the moon the reaper weary,

Piling sheaves in uplands airy,
Listening, whispers "Tis the fairy
Lady of Shalott."

Part II

There she weaves by night and day
A magic web with colours gay.
She has heard a whisper say,
A curse is on her if she stay
To look down to Camelot.
She knows not what the curse may be,
And so she weaveth steadily,
And little other care hath she,
The Lady of Shalott.

And moving thro' a mirror clear
That hangs before her all the year,
Shadows of the world appear.
There she sees the highway near
Winding down to Camelot:
There the river eddy whirls,
And there the surly village-churls,
And the red cloaks of market girls,
Pass onward from Shalott.

Sometimes a troop of damsels glad,
An abbot on an ambling pad,
Sometimes a curly shepherd-lad,
Or long-hair'd page in crimson clad,
Goes by to tower'd Camelot;
And sometimes thro' the mirror blue
The knights come riding two and two:
She hath no loyal knight and true,
The Lady of Shalott.

But in her web she still delights
To weave the mirror's magic sights,

For often thro' the silent nights
A funeral, with plumes and lights
And music, went to Camelot:
Or when the moon was overhead,
Came two young lovers lately wed:
"I am half sick of shadows," said
The Lady of Shalott. '

Part III

A bow-shot from her bower-eaves,
He rode between the barley-sheaves,
The sun came dazzling thro' the leaves,
And flamed upon the brazen greaves
Of bold Sir Lancelot.
A red-cross knight for ever kneel'd
To a lady in his shield,
That sparkled on the yellow field,
Beside remote Shalott.

The gemmy bridle glitter'd free,
Like to some branch of stars we see
Hung in the golden Galaxy.
The bridle bells rang merrily
As he rode down to Camelot:
And from his blazon'd baldric slung
A mighty silver bugle hung,
And as he rode his armour rung,
Beside remote Shalott.

All in the blue unclouded weather
Thick-jewell'd shone the saddle-leather,
The helmet and the helmet-feather
Burn'd like one burning flame together,
As he rode down to Camelot.
As often thro' the purple night,
Below the starry clusters bright,

Some bearded meteor, trailing light,
Moves over still Shalott.

His broad clear brow in sunlight glow'd;
On burnish'd hooves his war-horse trode;
From underneath his helmet flow'd
His coal-black curls as on he rode,
As he rode down to Camelot.
From the bank and from the river
He flash'd into the crystal mirror,
"Tirra lirra," by the river
Sang Sir Lancelot.

She left the web, she left the loom,
She made three paces thro' the room,
She saw the water-lily bloom,
She saw the helmet and the plume,
She look'd down to Camelot.
Out flew the web and floated wide;
The mirror crack'd from side to side;
"The curse is come upon me," cried
The Lady of Shalott.

Part IV

In the stormy east-wind straining,
The pale yellow woods were waning,
The broad stream in his banks complaining,
Heavily the low sky raining
Over tower'd Camelot;
Down she came and found a boat
Beneath a willow left afloat,
And round about the prow she wrote
The Lady of Shalott.

And down the river's dim expanse
Like some bold seer in a trance,
Seeing all his own mischance--

With a glassy countenance
Did she look to Camelot.
And at the closing of the day
She loosed the chain, and down she lay;
The broad stream bore her far away,
The Lady of Shalott.

Lying, robed in snowy white
That loosely flew to left and right--
The leaves upon her falling light--
Thro' the noises of the night
She floated down to Camelot:
And as the boat-head wound along
The willowy hills and fields among,
They heard her singing her last song,
The Lady of Shalott.

Heard a carol, mournful, holy,
Chanted loudly, chanted lowly,
Till her blood was frozen slowly,
And her eyes were darken'd wholly,
Turn'd to tower'd Camelot.
For ere she reach'd upon the tide
The first house by the water-side,
Singing in her song she died,
The Lady of Shalott.

Under tower and balcony,
By garden-wall and gallery,
A gleaming shape she floated by,
Dead-pale between the houses high,
Silent into Camelot.
Out upon the wharfs they came,
Knight and burgher, lord and dame,
And round the prow they read her name,
The Lady of Shalott.

Arthurian Poetry

Who is this? and what is here?
And in the lighted palace near
Died the sound of royal cheer;
And they cross'd themselves for fear,
All the knights at Camelot:
But Lancelot mused a little space;
He said, "She has a lovely face;
God in his mercy lend her grace,
The Lady of Shalott."

Tristram and Iseult

Matthew Arnold (1822-1888)
Matthew Arnold is sometimes referred to as the third great Victorian poet, after Tennyson and Robert Browning. His father was the famous Dr Thomas Arnold, the headmaster of Rugby School. He also wrote Arthurian poetry, the best known example being his long narrative poem *Tristram and Iseult*.

This tale was told in Part One, with the spelling of Tristram and Isolde. It starts with Tristram lying on his deathbed, awaiting the ship carrying Iseult back to him with a cure. He talks with his page, then the poem describes Tristram and his plight. He is married to Iseult of the Snow-White Hand, but the love of his life is the other Iseult with whom he drank the love potion.

Tristram

Tristram: "Is she not come? The messenger was sure—
Prop me upon the pillows once again—
Raise me, my page! this cannot long endure.
—Christ, what a night! how the sleet whips the pane!
What lights will those out to the northward be?"

The Page: "The lanterns of the fishing-boats at sea."

Tristram: "Soft—who is that, stands by the dying fire?"

The Page: "Iseult."

Tristram: "Ah! not the Iseult I desire."

What Knight is this so weak and pale,
Though the locks are yet brown on his noble head,
Propt on pillows in his bed,
Gazing seaward for the light
Of some ship that fights the gale
On this wild December night?
Over the sick man's feet is spread
A dark green forest-dress;
A gold harp leans against the bed,
Ruddy in the fire's light.
I know him by his harp of gold,
Famous in Arthur's court of old;
I know him by his forest-dress—
The peerless hunter, harper, knight,
Tristram of Lyoness.

Then he describes Iseult of the Snow-White hand, whom he is married to but does not love. She pines for him.

What Lady is this, whose silk attire
Gleams so rich in the light of the fire?
The ringlets on her shoulders lying
In their flitting lustre vying
With the clasp of burnish'd gold
Which her heavy robe doth hold.
Her looks are mild, her fingers slight
As the driven snow are white;
But her cheeks are sunk and pale.
Is it that the bleak sea-gale
Beating from the Atlantic sea
On this coast of Brittany,
Nips too keenly the sweet flower?
Is it that a deep fatigue
Hath come on her, a chilly fear,

Passing all her youthful hour
Spinning with her maidens here,
Listlessly through the window-bars
Gazing seawards many a league,
From her lonely shore-built tower,
While the knights are at the wars?
Or, perhaps, has her young heart
Felt already some deeper smart,
Of those that in secret the heart-strings rive,
Leaving her sunk and pale, though fair?
Who is this snowdrop by the sea? —
I know her by her mildness rare,
Her snow-white hands, her golden hair;
I know her by her rich silk dress,
And her fragile loveliness —
The sweetest Christian soul alive,
Iseult of Brittany.
Iseult of Brittany? —but where
Is that other Iseult fair,
That proud, first Iseult, Cornwall's queen?
She, whom Tristram's ship of yore
From Ireland to Cornwall bore,
To Tyntagel, to the side
Of King Marc, to be his bride?
She who, as they voyaged, quaff'd
With Tristram that spiced magic draught,
Which since then for ever rolls
Through their blood, and binds their souls,
Working love, but working teen? —.
There were two Iseults who did sway
Each her hour of Tristram's day;
But one possess'd his waning time,
The other his resplendent prime.
Behold her here, the patient flower,
Who possess'd his darker hour!
Iseult of the Snow-White Hand
Watches pale by Tristram's bed.

And so the poem unfolds. You will know the tale from Part One. If you would like to read more, then searching out Matthew Arnold's full poem will repay the effort.

La Belle Dame Sans Merci

John Keats (1795–1821)
John Keats was a qualified apothecary but he never actually practised medicine. He became one of the main Romantic poets of the early Nineteenth Century, along with Lord George Byron and Percy Bysshe Shelley.

With his poem, *La Belle Dame Sans Merci,* he created one of the finest Arthurian poems which inspired numerous paintings in the Victorian era. This ballad poem is a mere twelve stanzas, yet it creates a mysterious mood that evokes the days of chivalry and magic. It is about an unnamed narrator who comes upon an unnamed knight, close to death in a field. The knight says that he had met a mysterious damsel, perhaps of fairy blood. She seemed to love him and took him to a grotto and there induced a disturbing dream of all the knights, kings and princes that she had previously seduced – and who died.

He woke to find himself back on the road, all alone. It is an enigma, just ripe for being depicted by one of the great Pre-Raphaelite artists. Among those who painted it were Sir Frank Dicksee, Walter Crane and Frank Cadogan Cowper.

I

O What can ail thee, knight-at-arms,
Alone and palely loitering?
The sedge has wither'd from the lake,
And no birds sing.

II

O What can ail thee, knight-at-arms!
So haggard and so woe-begone?
The squirrel's granary is full,
And the harvest's done.

III

I see a lily on thy brow
With anguish moist and fever dew,
And on they cheeks a fading rose
Fast withered too.

IV

I met a lady in the meads,
Full beautiful – a faery's child,
Her hair was long, her foot was light,
And her eyes were wild.

V

I made a garland for her head,
And bracelets too, and fragrant zone;
She look'd at me as she did love,
And made sweet moan.

VI

I set her on my pacing steed,
And nothing else saw all day long,
For sidelong would she bend, and sing
A faery's song.

VII

She found me roots of relish sweet,
And honey wild, and manna dew,
And sure in language strange she said -
"I love thee true."

VIII

She took me to her elfin grot,
And there she wept, and sigh'd full sore,
And there I shut her wild wild eyes
With kisses four.

IX
And there she lulled me asleep,
And there I dream'd – Ah! Woe betide!
The latest dream I ever dream'd
On the cold hill's side.

X
I saw pale kings and princes too,
Pale warriors, death-pale were they all;
They cried – "La Belle Dame sans Merci
Hath thee in thrall!"

XI
I saw their starved lips in the gloam,
With horrid warning gaped wide,
And I awoke and found me here,
On the cold hill's side.

XII
And this is why I sojourn here,
Alone and palely loitering,
The sedge has wither'd from the lake,
And no birds sing.

The Black Tower

William Butler Yeats (1865-1939)
The Black Tower may be based on the tower in Ireland that Yeats bought in 1917, when he was 52 years old. This is the last poem that he wrote, composing it just a week before he died in France. It is considered Arthurian in tone and is quite haunting and beautiful.

> *Say that the men of the old black tower,*
> *Though they but feed as the goatherd feeds,*
> *Their money spent, their wine gone sour,*
> *Lack nothing that a soldier needs,*
> *That all are oath-bound men:*
> *Those banners come not in.*

Arthurian Poetry

There in the tomb stand the dead upright,
But winds come up from the shore:
They shake when the winds roar,
Old bones upon the mountain shake.

Those banners come to bribe or threaten,
Or whisper that a man's a fool
Who, when his own right king's forgotten,
Cares what king sets up his rule.
If he died long ago
Why do you dread us so?

There in the tomb drops the faint moonlight,
But wind comes up from the shore:
They shake when the winds roar,
Old bones upon the mountain shake.

The tower's old cook that must climb and clamber
Catching small birds in the dew of the morn
When we hale men lie stretched in slumber
Swears that he hears the king's great horn.
But he's a lying hound:
Stand we on guard oath-bound!

There in the tomb the dark grows blacker,
But wind comes up from the shore:
They shake when the winds roar,
Old bones upon the mountain shake.

The Waste Land

T.S. Eliot (1888-1965)
T.S. Eliot wrote *The Waste Land* in 1922 and later became the Nobel Laureate. Regarded as one of the most important poems of the Twentieth Century, it is a modernist poem, 434 lines long and loosely follows the Holy Grail legend and the Fisher King, hence the title, *The Waste Land*.

Chapter Nine

The Real Arthur

When Arthur learned that they were upon the march, he made over the charge of defending Britain unto his nephew Mordred and his Queen Guenevere, he himself with his army making for hamo's port, where he embarked with a fair breeze of wind.

Historia Regum Britanniae, *or*
History of the kings of Britain,
Geoffrey of Monmouth, 1135 AD

THERE are several questions that obsess many an Arthurian scholar and enthusiast. Was there ever a real King Arthur, or an historical person upon whom the whole saga was based? And can this person be identified in the historical record? Countless books have been written about the subject and people have forged careers on the basis of their research. The thing is that even today, we still do not know. There are those who say that he was simply a myth created when people needed such a hero, and others who are quite adamant not only that he existed but that he can be identified with certainty.

Emperor Magnus Maximus, one of the contenders.

The main candidates

The first contender, of course, has to be King Arthur himself. For centuries it was accepted that he was an actual King of Britain, or King of the Britons. Writers like Geoffrey of Monmouth had, after all, written extensively about him in his *Historia Regum Britanniae*, or *History of the*

Kings of Britain. It was only when the evidence for his existence was scrutinised that it was considered to be scanty. Then the idea that he was a mythical rather than an historical figure gained credence.

The difficulty is that the whole Arthurian saga seems to have been built up layer upon layer, almost century by century. The legend has grown in the telling, so to speak. If there was a true Arthur then what sort of a man was he? A warrior, a cavalry general, a warlord or a king?

It is an intriguing question.

Lucius Artorius Castus

This candidate was a Sarmatian cavalry officer of the mid-Third Century. This theory was first put forward by the historian Kemp Malone in 1924. More recently C. Scott Littleton and Linda Malcor have put forward their case for this being the true Arthur. Indeed, the 2004 film *King Arthur* was based on this premise.

The Sarmatians were from Scythia in the Roman Empire. This corresponds with modern day Southern Russia and the Balkans. Fabulous horsemen, they were used as cavalrymen. They also revered their swords and carried standards in the form of dragons. The comparison with the Pendragon name and the mounted swordsmen image is quite attractive, for one can see how it could equate with the idea of mounted knights.

Lucius Artorius Castus was a real person and there is evidence that he was a commander in the north of Britain. It is also known that he was called back to fight in Gaul, or modern France. His middle name, Artorius, is also quite similar to that of Arthur.

Riothamus

This candidate was a Romano-Briton who was active in the late Fifth Century, so the date is more in his favour if we are to accept that King Arthur was alive in the Fifth or Sixth Centuries. He was a commander who fought against the Goths and he is mentioned by the Sixth Century historian Jordanis as King of the Britons. He led an army of Britons against the Goths and was betrayed by Arvandus, the Roman Prefect of Gaul. He was defeated and killed.

The historian Geoffrey Ashe first put forward his theory that Riothamus was the real King Arthur in 1981. He postulates a plausible link between the betrayal of Riothanus by Arvandus and the betrayal of King Arthur by Mordred. He has expanded on the theory in his 1985 book, *The Discovery of King Arthur* and his 1987 book, *The Landscape of King Arthur*.

Aurelius Ambrosius

This candidate is also referred to as Ambrosius Aurelianus. He was a real Romano-Briton nobleman who had the title Dux Bellorum, which means Duke of Battles. He led the Britons against the Saxons after the Romans left Britain in 410 AD. It is thought that he may have been the commander at the Battle of Badon, which would indeed give him a good claim to be the historical Arthur.

Gildas mentions that he 'wore the purple,' meaning that he was effectively of royal rank.

Geoffrey of Monmouth mentions that he was a King of Britain but does not equate him with Arthur, implying again that he was an older brother of Uther Pendragon.

Magnus Maximus

This person was known in Welsh as Macsen Wledig. He was a Roman commander in Britain and successfully fought off invading Picts in north England. He usurped the Emperor Gratian in 383 AD to become the Western Roman Emperor, which position he held until 388 AD. He left Britain to fight in Gaul and invaded Italy where he was defeated at the Battle of the Save in 388 AD. He was subsequently captured and executed at Aqulieia, a city at the head of the Adriatic.

He has drifted into Welsh legends and is remembered in *The Mabinogian* in the *The Dream of Macsen Wledig*. In this he has a dream of a beautiful woman and searches the world for her, finding her in Wales. He marries her and gives her father sovereignty of Britain.

The Real Arthur

Arthun, son of Magnus Maximus and Athwrys of Glywyssing and Gwent

An interesting and controversial theory has been proposed by amateur historians Alan Wilson and Baram Blackett in their 1998 book, *The Holy Kingdom*, that there were in fact two King Arthurs. One was Arthun, whom they refer to as King Arthur 1. He lived in the late Fourth Century and was the son of Magnus Maximus. The second was Athwrys of Glywyssing and Gwent, whom they refer to as King Arthur 2. Their argument is that these two King Arthurs shared ancestry back to King Brutus and to the Holy Family itself. The suggestion is that the two have been amalgamated into the single character of King Arthur.

The theories make interesting reading, but they are not accepted by academe.

Owain Ddantgwyn

This person was King of Powys in about 500 AD. Graham Phillips and Martin Keatman wrote a book, *King Arthur: The True Story* in 1992. They very persuasively suggest that Owain Ddantgwyn assumed the title 'Arthur,' and that he ruled where King Arthur was supposed to have lived and ruled. He was a king at the time of the Battle of Badon.

They suggest that Arthur almost certainly means 'the Bear'. They propose that rather than the name being derived from a Latin name like Artorius, that it could have been from *'arth,'* meaning bear, a nickname reference to his warrior bearing. This would fit with the mention of his son Cuneglasus by Gildas, whom he calls the 'charioteer of the Bear's stronghold.'

Further, they have worked out that his nephew was Maglocunas, who according to Gildas gained his kingdom by overthrowing his uncle. Maglocunas could, therefore, have been transformed into Mordred who attempted to usurp King Arthur's throne.

Arthnou

This candidate was a Prince of Tintagel in the Sixth Century. Not much is known about him but a piece of slate, referred to as 'the Arthur Stone,' was found at Tintagel in 1998. It is in Latin and says that, 'Artognou, father of a descendent of Coll, has had this built'.

This Coll may well be the Old King Cole of nursery rhyme fame. There are several possible King Coles from different parts of the country. All three could be associated with this Arthnou.

Artognou would be pronounced Arthnou. It is not much to go on but it is something tangible.

Artur Mac Aidan

This theory is that Arthur was Artur Mac Aidan, the son of King Aidan Mac Gabran, who ruled in Dalriada (or modern day Argyll) around 570 AD. He was a generalissimo who led the Scots and the Britons against pagan invaders. It is said that he used an old Roman fort called Camelon near Falkirk, which of course bears a similarity to Camelot. He died in battle in 582 AD fighting against the Picts near the River Allan, which is also known as Camallan. This also bears a resemblance to Camlann. He had a sister called Morgan, as did King Arthur, and he was contemporary with Myrddin Wyllt, who may later have been identified as Merlin.

Finally, when he died he was buried on an island in the River Forth that was called Invalone. Perhaps it is just another coincidence, but its name does bear a resemblance to the Isle of Avalon. This is quiet a tempting collection of similar names but the part of the country and the enemies that he fought are not consistent with the tales that the writers of the Arthurian saga have given us.

Was King Arthur a real King, or even an actual person? What do you think?

Chapter Ten

King Arthur in Popular Culture

They were always having grand tournaments there at Camelot; and very stirring and picturesque and ridiculous human bull-fights they were, too, but just a little wearisome to the practical mind.
A Connecticut Yankee at the Court of King Arthur,
Mark Twain, 1889

KING Arthur may or may not have ever existed in fact. He certainly exists in the public imagination, if the number of books, films, video games and television programmes relating to him is anything to go by. We simply do not seem to be able to get enough of him, or of his adventurous Knights of the Round Table.

New Camelot JFK.

Literature

We looked at the literary origins of the tales of King Arthur earlier in the book. It did not end with Tennyson, of course. Many writers have tried their hand at retelling the tales, or at creating new works of fiction, using Camelot or the Arthurian era as a backdrop for their work.

A Connecticut Yankee at the Court of King Arthur

This comic novel by Samuel L. Clemens (1835-1910), better known as Mark Twain, was published in 1889. It is the tale of Hank Morgan, a Nineteenth Century citizen of Hartford, Connecticut, who is mysteriously transported to Camelot following a head injury with a crow bar. Accepting that he has time-travelled he decides to use his

A modern American Camelot

John Fitzgerald Kennedy (1917-1963), often simply referred to as JFK, was the 35th President of the USA. His presidency lasted for 1,000 days, but was cut short when he was fatally wounded by an assassin's bullet on the 22nd of November, 1963 as he rode in an open-topped limousine through the streets of Dallas, Texas. The man accused of the assassination, Lee Harvey Oswald, was himself assassinated by Jack Ruby two days later.

Shortly after his state funeral, JFK's widow, Jacqueline Kennedy, known fondly as Jackie, gave an interview to Theodore White, a journalist, for an article to be featured in *Life* magazine. She compared her husband's presidency with the Camelot of King Arthur. It was a time of hope, when men were gallant, great deeds were done and when the White House was a place graced by writers, poets and artists. She thought that her husband was a heroic figure, like a knight of old.

Apparently, during the interview she played her husband's favourite song, the closing song of the Broadway musical *Camelot*.

In his article, Theodore White put forward the association between King Arthur's court and the Presidency of John F. Kennedy, calling it an American Camelot. It was an image that the American public and the world seemed to appreciate. After all, his was a life cut short by a violent death; the most powerful man in the world killed by a cowardly lone assassin shooting from cover.

Jackie Kennedy herself was a beautiful woman, a fitting 'First Lady' of the USA for the handsome President. She later married the shipping tycoon Aristotle Onassis and had a successful career in publishing in her own right. She maintained dignity to the end of her days.

From such things are legends made.

modern day knowledge to improve matters in the Sixth Century and rise to the top of the social tree. He is hampered, however, by the ill will and machinations of the charlatan, Merlin.

A Connecticut Yankee at the Court of King Arthur.

Behind the humour Twain creates a social satire and pokes fun at the concept of chivalry and the Victorian romanticization of the Middle Ages.

That Hideous Strength

This is the last of three Christian-based science fiction novels, known collectively as *The Space Trilogy*, by C.S. Lewis (1898-1963), the author of *The Chronicles of Narnia*. The hero of the three tales is Dr Elwin Ransom, a philologist. He fights demonic forces and is revealed to be the Pendragon, the heir of King Arthur.

The Acts of King Arthur and His Noble Knights

This is a retelling of the Arthurian saga by John Steinbeck (1902-1963), the 1962 Nobel Laureate, which was published in 1976. It is based upon the Winchester manuscript of Malory's *Le Morte d'Arthur*.

Sword at Sunset

Rosemary Sutcliffe (1920-1992) wrote this novel about Artos, using Nennius' *History of the Britons* as the base. It is part of her famous *Eagle of the Ninth* series of books. It places Artos, a cavalry commander, in the era when the Romans had left Britain and is a wonderfully atmospheric interpretation of the Arthur story.

The Crimson Chalice

Victor Canning (1911-1986) wrote three Arthurian novels – *The Crimson Chalice* in 1976, *The Circle of the Gods* in 1977 and *The Immortal Wound* in 1978. They were collectively published as *The Crimson Chalice* to tell the story of Arturo. It is not a re-telling but a series of novels based on the Arthur legend.

The Mists of Avalon

This is a novel by Marion Zimmer Bradley (1930-1999) which is a retelling of the Arthurian legends from the point of view of the female characters. It follows Morgaine (Morgan le Fay), a priestess fighting to save the mother religion of the Celts from the paternalistic Christian religion. It also focuses on Gwenhwyfar, Viviene, Morgause and Igrayne.

It was later developed into the Avalon series.

The Warlord Chronicles

Bernard Cornwell is a well known historical novelist whose Napoleonic novels about Richard Sharpe have reached cult status.

He has produced several series of novels set in different epochs. *The Warlord Chronicles* are based in Arthurian, post-Roman Britain. *The Winter King* is the first, published in 1995. It tells of how Uther, the High King of Britain, dies and leaves the kingdom to his heir, Mordred. His uncle is Arthur, who wages war against other kingdoms on his behalf. The second novel, *The Enemy of God*, published in 1996, tells of how Arthur has united the kingdoms to face the common enemy, the Saxons. The final novel, *Excalibur: A Novel of Arthur* wonderfully completes the story.

Another series entitled *The Grail Quest* transposes a quest for the Holy Grail to the Fourteenth Century and the Hundred Years War. The one word titles, *Harlequin* (2000), *Vagabond* (2002) and *Heretic* (2003) are all splendid tales by a master of his craft.

The Death of King Arthur

Peter Ackroyd published a retelling of Malory's *Le Morte d'Arthur* in 2010 modern English.

There are literally hundreds of novels based on the Arthurian story, but these should be enough to whet the appetite of interested readers.

Films

The film industry has always viewed the popularity of the Arthurian tales as good reason to launch another film. From the silent era to the first colour films to the blockbusters of today, there have been films about Arthur, his knights, the Holy Grail and about the great wizard, Merlin.

Silent movies

Parcifal

This was a two reel film produced in 1904, intended to be played to accompanying records of the opera by Richard Wagner.

The Quest for the Holy Grail

This was a silent movie based on the Grail legend. Sadly, it seems to be among the seventy per cent of silent movies that have been destroyed.

Modern movies

A Connecticut Yankee at the Court of King Arthur

This was a musical adaptation of Mark Twain's 1889 novel, from Paramount. It starred Bing Crosby as Hank Martin, or Sir Boss; Sir

Cedric Hardwyke as King Arthur; William Bendix as Sir Sagramore; Rhonda Fleming as Asilande de Cartoise; Murvyn Vye as Merlin and Virginia Field as Morgan le Fay.

Knights of the Round Table

This was made in 1953 by MGM, starring Robert Taylor, who had just made Ivanhoe, as Sir Lancelot. It also starred Ava Gardner as Guinevere, Mel Ferrer as King Arthur and Stanley Baker as Mordred.

The Black Knight

This was made by Warwick Films in 1954, starring Alan Ladd as the hero who attempts to save the Lady Linet and King Arthur from the evil conspirators played by Peter Cushing and Patrick Troughton.

Cushing would later become a stalwart of British horror movies and a regular Sherlock Holmes. Patrick Troughton would become the second Dr Who.

The Sword in the Stone

This is the famous 1963 Disney animation, based on T.H. White's first book in his *Once and Future King* collection. It is based upon Merlin's teaching of the young Arthur, known as Wart.

Camelot

This is a 1967 film adaptation of the musical of the same name, starring Richard Harris as King Arthur, Vanessa Redgrave as Queen Guinevere and Franco Nero as Sir Lancelot. It won three Academy Awards, although none for acting.

The last song was reported to be John F. Kennedy's favourite.

Gawain and the Green Knight

This was a film of the poem *Sir Gawain and the Green Knight*, made in 1973 by United Artists, starring Murray Head as Sir Gawain and Nigel Green as the Green Knight.

King Arthur in Popular Culture

Monty Python and the Holy Grail

This was a hilarious film made in 1974, featuring the Monty Python team of Graham Chapman, John Cleese, Terry Jones, Michael Palin, Eric Idle and Terry Gilliam.

Excalibur

This is a 1983 film based on Malory's *Le Morte d'Arthur*. It stars Nigel Terry as King Arthur, Nicholas Clay as Lancelot, Cherie Lunghi as Guinevere, Helen Mirren as Morgana, Liam Neeson as Gawain, Patrick Stewart as Leodegraunce and Nicol Williamson as Merlin. The story of course revolves around the magical sword, Excalibur.

Sword of the Valiant

This was a remake of the 1973 movie *Gawain and the Green Knight* in 1984, starring Miles O'Keefe as Sir Gawain, Sean Connery as the Green Knight, and Robert Hardy as Bertilak.

First Knight

This is a 1993 film from Columbia, starring Sean Connery as King Arthur, Richard Gere as Lancelot, Julia Ormond as Guinevere and Ben Cross as Malagant. It is based on the Twelfth Century works of Chrétien de Troyes.

King Arthur

This is a 2004 film from Touchstone, starring Clive Owen as Arthur, Ioan Gruffudd as Lancelot and Keira Knightley as Guinevere. Arthur is a Roman officer rather than a king. It is set in Roman Britain and attempts to portray the period and the tale in the light of archaeological evidence. It is quite a departure from the traditional King Arthur.

Indiana Jones and the Last Crusade

This is the third film in the series of movies made about the all-American archaeology professor and adventurer, Indiana Jones. All of them have taken pulp fiction and amalgamated them with the matinee type of adventure movies of the 1930s and 1940s. This one, made in 1989 and set in 1938 sends Indiana Jones off in search of his father who has been kidnapped by Nazis. They want to obtain the Holy Grail. The film is a splendid adventure that includes much of the Quest for the Holy Grail, including the ancient knight whose purpose is to guard the Grail. He is an allusion, of course, to the Fisher King.

Television

Television has always been a fruitful medium for the tales of King Arthur or his knights. Children's television in the 1950s and 1960s had regular half-hour slots for several series, including Ivanhoe, featuring a young Roger Moore, Robin Hood, featuring Richard Green, William Tell, featuring Conrad Phillips and, of course, the many western series that were so popular then.

The Adventures of Sir Lancelot

This series ran for thirty episodes in 1956 and 1957. It featured William Russell as Sir Lancelot, Ronald Leigh-Hunt as King Arthur, Jane Hylton as Queen Guinevere and Cyril Smith as Merlin. It was a wonderful swash-buckling series.

William Russell would go on to become one of the first Dr Who assistants, playing Ian, the action man teacher.

Arthur of the Britons

This was a British television show that ran for two series in 1972 and 1973. It featured Oliver Tobias as Arthur, Brian Blessed as Mark of Cornwall, Michael Gothard as Kai, and Rupert Davies as Cerdig, the Chief of the Saxons.

Merlin

This is a British television show made by the BBC that started in 2008 and is now in its fourth series. It is about the youthful Merlin who comes to Uther Pendragon's court and finds that magic is outlawed. As a Dragon Lord he knows that he must preserve the ancient lore and he attempts to conceal his magical abilities while protecting his master, Prince Arthur – who becomes King Arthur in the fourth series – from all sorts of harm, often magical. Merlin's mentor is the court physician Gaius, played by Richard Wilson.

It features Colin Morgan who plays Merlin with great zest, Bradley James as Arthur, a strong, arrogant but deeply honourable character and Angel Coulby as Guinevere or Gwen, a servant for whom Arthur has feelings. Katie McGrath is an excellent Morgana and Anthony Head was a headstrong, stubborn Uther Pendragon.

It is excellent Saturday evening entertainment.

Camelot

This is a television series that was first shown in 2011, made by Startz and GK-TV. It attempts to portray an authentic Dark Ages Arthur. Joe Fiennes plays Merlin, Jamie Campbell Bower plays King Arthur, Eva Green plays Morgan, Tamsin Egertin plays Guinevere and Claire Forlani plays Igrayne.

Superheroes

Every age demands its heroes. In America in the early Twentieth Century the comic industry developed from the strip cartoons in the daily newspapers. All manner of heroes were produced, but in 1932 DC Comics produced *Superman, the Man of Steel*. An alien from the doomed planet of Krypton, he was sent to Earth by his father Jo-El just before his planet was about to explode. On Earth his incredibly dense atomic structure gave him prodigious powers. He was invulnerable, had super strength, x-ray vision and could fly. He became a righter of wrongs just like King Arthur of the olden days. With god-like powers he still had a weakness, however. If exposed to radioactive Kryptonite, which appeared on Earth in the occasional meteorite, he would lose his powers and become as weak as a kitten. Indeed, kryptonite was potentially fatal.

After Superman came a whole legion of superheroes from *DC Comics*. Batman, The Flash, Green Lantern and Wonder Woman. And eventually from their rival *Marvel Comics* came Spiderman, Thor, Ironman and X-Men, to name but a few. With the exception of Batman who relied on superior intelligence, advanced gadgetry and old fashioned heroic daring-do, they all had super powers. Their purpose was to fight crime and evil wherever in the universe it was found.

It is tempting to say that they were the direct descendents of King Arthur and his Knights of the Round Table. After all, many of them joined together to fight evil. The Justice League of America, X-Men and the Fantastic Four used their joint powers and abilities, rather like the Knights of the Round Table.

Yet if one cannot claim that they are inspired by the older heroes one can say that King Arthur and some of his knights have found themselves reborn to fight evil alongside some of their modern counterparts. *DC Comics* have often used Camelot as a background to stories and have either had characters go back in time or have brought King Arthur or certain of his knights forward.

In 1941, *DC Comics* introduced the character of the Shining Knight, or Sir Justin of Camelot. By a magical spell he had ended up in suspended animation for 1,500 years until awakened in the modern era to do what a knight of Camelot should. That is, fight evil wherever he saw it. And of course, in keeping with modern era necessity, he had an alter ego or secret identity as Justin Arthur.

Marvel Comics have also updated the legends and produced *The Excalibur* series and *The Knights of Pendragon*. And DC Comics have explored the legend that King Arthur and his knights are only sleeping and will come back when they are most needed. In *Camelot 3000*, a twelve issue series in the 1980s, King Arthur, Merlin and the Knights of the Round Table were all reincarnated to fight an alien menace that threatens the overpopulated Earth in the year 3000 AD. You may have guessed it; the menace was orchestrated by Morgan le Fay.

Truly, it seems that King Arthur will always be with us.

Bibliography

Ackroyd, P. *The Death of King Arthur*, Penguin, 2010

Couch, D. *William Marshal – Knighthood, War and Chivalry, 1147-1219*, Longman, 2nd edition, 2002

Cross, P. *The Knight in Medieval England 1000-1400*, Alan Sutton, 1993

de Camp, L.S. & C.C. *Citadels of Mystery*, Fontana Books, 1973

Gidlow, C. *The Reign of Arthur*, Sutton Publishing, 2004

Gidlow, C. *Revealing King Arthur*, The History Press, 2010

Green, R, L. *King Arthur and his Knights of the Round Table*, Penguin Books, 1953

Hardyman, C. *Malory – The Life and Times of King Arthur's Chronicler*, Harper Perennial, 2006

Kaeuper, R.W. *Chivalry and Violence in Medieval Europe*, Oxford University Press, 1999

Keen, M. *Chivalry*, Yale University Press, 1984

Lupack, A. *Oxford Guide to Arthurian Literature and Legend*, Oxford University Press, 2007

Malory, T., edited by Vinaver, E. *Malory Works*, Oxford University Press, 1966

Monmouth, G., translated by Evans, S. *History of the Kings of England or Historia Regum Brittaniae*, eBook

Nennius, translated by Giles, J.A. *History of the Britons*, Dodo Press, 2007

Phillips, G & Keatman, M. *King Arthur: The True Story*, Century, 1992

Propp, V., translated by Scott, L. Morphology of the Folktale, University of Texas 20th edition, 2009

Tennyson, A. *The Works of Alfred Lord Tennyson*, Macmillan and Co, 1885

White, T.H. *Once and Future King, The*, Fontana Books, 1979

White, T.H. *Book of Merlyn, The*, Fontana Books, 1978

Wood, M. *In Search of the Dark Ages*, BBC Books, 1981

Wood, M. *In Search of England*, Penguin Books, 1999

Index

Index